Old engraving showing Buittle Place before it was restored.

THE CASTLES OF
SOUTH-WEST SCOTLAND

Mike Salter

FOLLY PUBLICATIONS

ACKNOWLEDGEMENTS

The illustrations in this book are mostly the product of the author's own site surveys in 1977-86 and 1993. The plans have been redrawn from his field notes and drawings and are reproduced to scales of 1:400, 1:800, 1:1250, and 1:2000. The author also drew the sketches and maps and took most of the photographs. The old prints are reproduced from originals in his collection. Max Barfield provided computer facilities and she and her mother Anne Wilson checked the text. Thanks are due to Charles Henderson of Auchtermuchty in Fife who is building up a collection of pictures of all the castles in Scotland. He provided a number of photographs at very short notice including the colour picture of Isle of Whithorn Castle on the back of the cover and black and white pictures of Auchan, Auchness, Cassencarrie, Corsewall, Cruggleton, Dargarvel, Galdenoch, Killasser, and Sorbie. His pictures of Garrion and Jerviswood have been turned by the author into sketches. In the section on Galloway the pictures of the towers at Drumcoltran, Isle of Whithorn and the Old Place of Mochrum are derived from colour photographs taken by Charles Walton. Alan Sorenson, John Wright, and Peter Presford also need to be thanked for advice and information.

AUTHOR'S NOTES

Of all the Folly Publications books yet produced this has been the longest to come to fruition in the sense that material for Galloway, Ayrshire and Renfrewshire was originally prepared in three separate manuscripts ten years ago. It is now hoped that eventually there will be four further companion volumes to cover all the Scottish castellated buildings up to the late 17th century about which details are available.

By far the most difficult part in the production of this book was deciding what boundaries and district names to use in view of the widesweeping changes made in 1974. For this volume it was decided to retain the old county boundaries and names as they made conveniently sized units for gazetteers. Their names are still familiar and they are used in almost all the existing published material on Scottish castles.

Each of the main levels of a building is called a storey in this book, the basement or ground level room being the first storey. Sleeping lofts squeezed under vaults are usually treated as separate storeys. Attics entirely within roof spaces are generally mentioned separately, a building being thus of so many storeys plus an attic.

It is recommended that visitors use the Ordnance Survey 1:50,000 scale maps to find monuments. Grid References are given in the gazetteers. Where A.M. precedes the grid reference the building is maintained in a reasonable condition as an ancient monument. An additional * indicates that there are set opening hours and/or an admission fee payable. The other maintained ruins can be freely visited at any time. Most of the unmaintained sites can be visited but some are in a dangerous condition so take care. Ask permission where appropriate (it will rarely be refused) and remember to close gates, keep dogs on leads, and leave the monuments in the condition you find them. Owners of habitable buildings will occasionally show visitors around, especially if you are able to make an appointment in advance.

All measurements quoted in the text and the scales on the plans are metric as the buildings have been measured in metres. Additional dimensions and scales in feet and inches would have taken up too much space. For those who feel the need to make a conversion 3 metres is fractionally under 10 feet. Unless specifically stated as otherwise all dimensions are external at or near the ground level.

I.S.B.N. 1 871731 16 X

Copyright 1993 by Mike Salter. First published November 1993.
Folly Publications, Folly Cottage, 151 West Malvern Rd, Malvern, Worcs, WR14 4AY.
Printed by Severnside Printers, Bridge House, Upton-upon-Severn, Worcs, WR8 OHG

Old print of Auchan Castle

CONTENTS

Glossary of Terms   Page   4

Introduction   Page   5

Gazetteer of Castles in Ayrshire   Page   20

Gazetteer of Castles in Dumfriesshire   Page   60

Gazetteer of Castles in Galloway   Page   86

Gazetteer of Castles in Lanark & Renfrew   Page   122

Further Reading   Page   152

Maps and notes on mottes occur at the end of each gazetteer.

A GLOSSARY OF TERMS

Ashlar	- Masonry of blocks with even faces and square edges.
Attic	- A topmost storey entirely with a gabled roof.
Aumbry	- A recess or cupboard for storage.
Bailey	- A defensible space enclosed by a wall or palisade and a ditch.
Barbican	- A building or enclosure defending a castle entrance.
Barmkin	- An enclosure, usually of modest size and defensive strength.
Bartizan	- A turret corbelled out from a wall, usually at the summit.
Brattice	- A projection from a wall top providing machicolations.
Caphouse	- Small square gabled space over a staircase or round projection.
Cartouche	- Tablet with ornate frame and usually heraldry and an inscription.
Commendator	- Layman holding abbey revenues in trust when there is no Abbot.
Corbel	- A projecting bracket supporting other stonework or timbers.
Crannog	- A small artificial island occupied as a dwelling.
Crow Steps	- Squared stones forming steps upon a gable.
Curtain Wall	- A high enclosing stone wall around a bailey.
Dormer Window	- A window standing up vertically from the slope of a roof.
Gunloop	- An opening for firearm with an external splay. See also shot-hole.
Hall House	- Defensible two storey building containing a hall above a basement.
Harling	- Or Roughcast. Plaster with gravel or other coarse aggregate.
Hood Mould	- A projecting moulding above an arch or lintel to throw off water.
Jamb	- The side of a doorway, window, or other opening.
Keep	- A citadel or ultimate strongpoint. Originally called a donjon.
Light	- A compartment of a window.
Loop	- A small opening to admit light or for the discharge of missiles.
Machicolation	- A slot for dropping stones or shooting missiles at assailants.
Moat	- A ditch, water filled or dry, around an enclosure.
Motte	- A steeply sided flat topped mound, usually mostly man-made.
Moulding	- An ornament of continuous section.
Mullion	- A vertical member dividing the lights of a window.
Ogival Arch	- An arch of oriental origin with both convex and concave curves.
Oriel	- A bay window projecting out from a wall above ground level.
Palace	- An old Scottish term for a two storey hall block.
Parapet	- A wall for protection at any sudden drop.
Pediment	- A small gable over a doorway or window, especially a dormer.
Peel	- Originally a palisaded court. Later a stone tower house.
Pilaster	- A flat buttress. A common feature of 12th-13th century buildings
Pit Prison	- A dark prison only reached by a hatch in a vault.
Plinth	- The projecting base of a wall. It may be battered or stepped.
Portcullis	- A wooden gate designed to rise and fall in vertical grooves.
Postern	- A secondary gateway or doorway. A back entrance.
Quoin	- Dressed (i.e. carefully shaped) stone at a corner of a building.
Rebate	- Rectangular section cut out of a masonry edge usually for a door.
Rib Vault	- A vault supported by ribs or decorated with them.
Scale-and-platt Staircase	- Staircase with short straight flights and turns at landings.
Skewputt	- Bottom bracket of a gable upstanding above a roof.
Shot-hole	- A small round hole in an outer wall face for discharging firearms.
Tower House	- Self contained house with the main rooms stacked vertically.
Yett	- A strong hinged gate made of interwoven iron bars.
Wall-walk	- A walkway on top of a wall, protected by a parapet.
Ward	- A stone walled defensive enclosure.

INTRODUCTION

The word castle came into use in Britain in the 11th century. It was recognised that the many privately owned defensible residences with which William, Duke of Normandy and his followers had filled England after their conquest of that country in 1066, represented something new both in function and appearence. Strategically positioned castles allowed the new Norman landowning class to establish their rule over the Saxon populace. Under a new system called feudalism the king granted groups of manors to tenants-in-chief in return for military service each year by the tenant and his knights. Tenants in turn gave land to their knights on the same basis.

Castles and feudalism were introduced to SW Scotland in the time of King David I. He ruled Strathclyde from 1107 to 1124 under his brother Alexander I, and then himself ruled the whole kingdom until 1153. David lived much of his early life in England under the capable rule of Henry I and became Earl of Huntingdon as a result of his marriage in 1113. David I saw the advantages of feudalism over the system previously used in Scotland where the King was no more than a noble with a special title, having little power outside his own domain. The imposition of the new system increased his power and provided him with a regular army, although many districts, like Galloway, remained semi-independent. David brought up knights from England and gave them estates in the Clyde valley and the northern half of what later became the county of Ayr on this basis. Among them were Walter Fitz-Alan and Hugh de Morville who became the ancestors of the Stewarts and Cunninghames respectively, and the Montgomeries and Flemings. These lords then built castles to protect themselves and their goods, to control the approaches to their lands, and as symbols of lordly rank.

Except for the royal castles on volcanic crags at Edinburgh, Stirling, and Dumbarton the early castles in Scotland were not generally buildings of mortared stone. For the building in stone several years of peaceful conditions would be needed plus far more masons than were then available. Instead they were hastily made constructions of earth and wood. Commonly earth was dug from a circular ditch and piled within it to form a mound called a motte on which was erected a wooden house or tower forming the lord's residence within a small palisaded enclosure. There might be on one side or around the motte a base court or bailey containing a hall, chapel, kitchen, stables, barns, workshops, etc, normally defended by a rampart or ditch. Not many Scottish mottes have baileys and the few that do can be assumed to be places of some importance held by men of the highest rank. No timber buildings have survived but excavations have revealed enough traces of them to give an idea of what they were like. The surviving earthworks vary greatly in size and shape. Wherever possible natural features such as spurs, promontories, and glacial mounds might be given a minimal amount of scarping and heightening to produce the required shape. On low lying sites by rivers or marshes ditches might be water filled either permanently or seasonally. A few smaller mottes may have only been temporary observation posts. An alternative to the motte is the ringwork, a hybrid type not common in Scotland between a motte and a bailey with high banks around a modestly sized enclosure.

Kilmacolm Motte

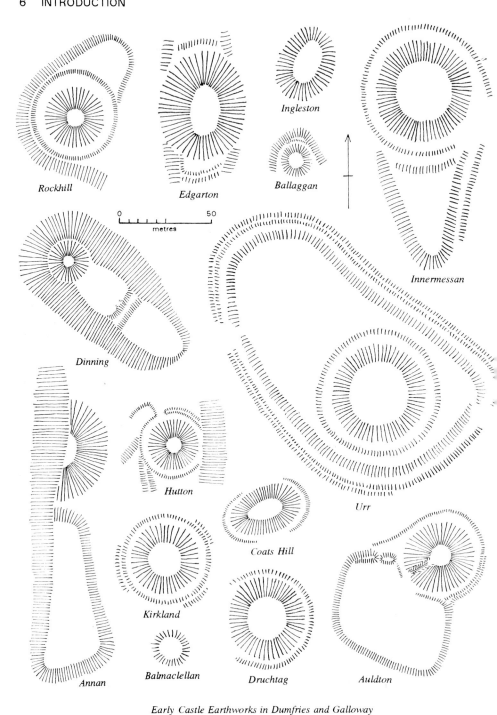

Early Castle Earthworks in Dumfries and Galloway

There was resistance to the new order from the old Gaelic and Norse chiefs. The natives of Galloway were particularly hostile to the Anglo-Normans with their alien culture and language, rising in rebellion in 1160 and 1174. The earliest true castle in that province was probably that built by Malcolm IV at Kirkcudbright c1160 after which the local rulers seem to have adopted them. A date of c1165-95 is thus likely for most of the earthworks in Galloway and indeed these of SW Scotland in general except for a few in the Clyde Valley and one or two in Ayrshire which are perhaps earlier. There is some evidence to suggest that the timber buildings on some of these sites continued to be occupied and kept in repair until at least the 14th century if not later, for as we shall presently see stone castles remained rare until the 15th century.

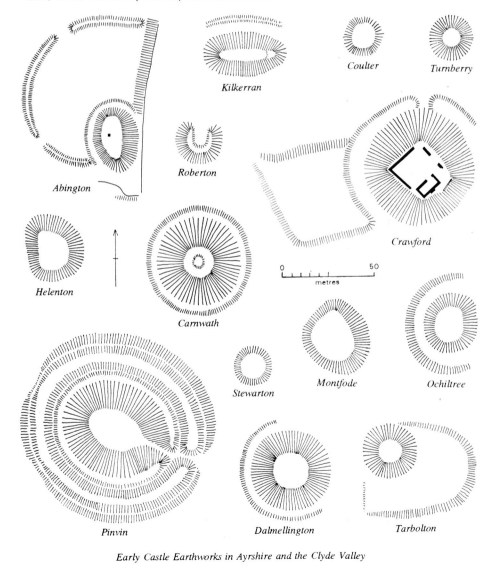

Early Castle Earthworks in Ayrshire and the Clyde Valley

Under Alexander II (1214-49) and Alexander III (1249-86) Scotland enjoyed the sort of prosperity that would not return for centuries. Several castles have remains of stone buildings from this period. Unfortunately none of them can be precisely dated and all of them were slighted to prevent them being occupied by the English during the reigns of Robert I (the Bruce 1306-29) and David II (1329-71). Those at the former county towns of Ayr (p24), Wigtown (p105) and Kirkcudbright (p118) were not rebuilt and have vanished, although we know from excavations that Kirkcudbright had a small rectangular court with round corner towers and a twin towered gatehouse. Footings also remain of a twin towered gatehouse at Buittle (p89), another castle never restored. Ayr Castle is said to have been triangular with round corner towers.

Southern Ayrshire was originally part of Galloway but was made into a separate Earldom of Carrick in the early 13th century with Turnberry Castle as its chief seat (p58). This building also seems to have been a ruin since slighting c1310 but it has some interesting features, notably an enclosed dock for ships below the small inner court which has a fragment of an apartment block, a square tower by the gate to the outer court, and a D-shaped tower keep facing to landward. Loch Doon (p48), on the border between Galloway and Carrick, and Cruggleton (p96) on the Galloway coast had small polygonal stone walled courts. Little remains of the latter but most of the wall at Loch Doon survives, having been rebuilt on the shore to save it from being submerged by a lake level rise. The lost castle of Kiers (p43) may have been similar.

The Keep, Bothwell Castle

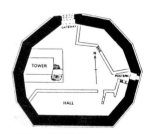

Plan of Loch Doon Castle

Plan of Tibbers Castle

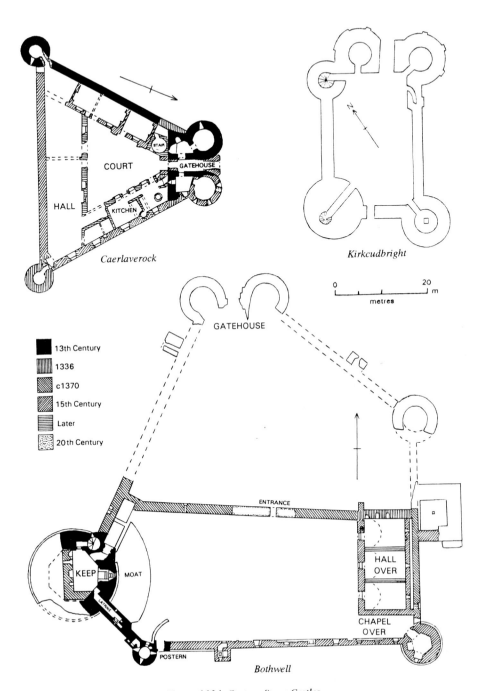

Caerlaverock

Kirkcudbright

GATEHOUSE

0   20
metres   m

COURT

HALL

KITCHEN

STAIR

GATEHOUSE

■ 13th Century

▨ 1336

▧ c1370

▨ 15th Century

▤ Later

▦ 20th Century

ENTRANCE

KEEP   MOAT

HALL OVER

CHAPEL OVER

POSTERN

Bothwell

Plans of 13th Century Stone Castles

There are remains of the basements of early tower houses tentatively dated to the late 13th century at Dunure (p37) and Rowallan (p53-4). Footings of a tower with fragments of a bailey wall of uncertain date remain at Duchal (p137). More interesting are the courtyards with gatehouses at Ardrossan (p21-2) and Dundonald (p36). Both were subsequently heavily rebuilt in the late 14th century when the gatehouses containing the lord's private rooms were made still more private by blocking the gateway passages and providing new courtyard gateways alongside. The Ardrossan gatehouse is rectangular, but that at Dundonald had a pair of shallow round fronts i.e. was effectively formed of two large D-shaped towers flanking a passage.

Craigie (p30) has a much rebuilt 13th century hall house with the parapet of the original wall-walk embedded in later work. It contained just a hall above a storage basement. Little remains of a larger structure of this type at Terringzean (p56). The single most impressive remaining structure of the whole of this period in South-West Scotland, however is the remaining half of the Murrays' huge four storey round tower keep at Bothwell (p125-7) thought to have been modelled on that of Coucy in France built by Alexander III's brother-in-law. The walls are ashlar faced like those at Loch Doon and Kirkcudbright and the architectural details are fine. This keep was intended to stand at one corner of a pentagonal court with a twin round towered gatehouse at another corner and round towers on the others, as at the contemporary castle of Kildrummy forming the seat of the Earldom of Mar, but only a short length of walling connecting the keep to a small corner tower seems to have been built above the footings in the initial campaign. Only this castle as originally laid out and that of Turnberry would have been large enough to rival the splendid fortresses built by 13th century lords in England and France. None of these early castles retain any domestic apartments but the rooms in the keeps and flanking towers must have been supplemented by wooden framed halls and other lean-to timber framed buildings.

The Scots did not indulge in much castle-building between the death of Alexander III's infant grand-daughter in 1290 and the accession of Robert II, the first of the Stewarts, in 1371. As noted above the existing castles were all destroyed to prevent them being used by the English. Two castles in Dumfriesshire, Caerlaverock (p65) and Tibbers (p83) are thought to have been built in the 1290s by Scots lords persuaded or forced into supporting Edward I of England in his campaign to subjugate Scotland. Both have small courts, triangular (with a wet moat) at Caerlaverock and rectangular at Tibbers, with twin towered gatehouses and round corner towers. Both were destroyed by the Scots and only Caerlaverock was subsequently restored. Edward I built a rectangular palisaded court called a peel at Lochmaben (p74) which in the 1360s was refortified by Edward III with thick walls and the rare feature of a canal to the loch to allow boats to be brought under the walls. The massively walled court at Auchan (p61) may also be of this period. A hall at Hestan (p101) may be of c1340.

The large L-shaped tower house built at Edinburgh Castle by David II in the 1360s seems to have formed the model for a number of large and massively walled plain rectangular towers built in SW Scotland in the period 1370-1400. The great lords of Northern England at this time were building castles with four ranges of apartments around a central court as at Bolton. However, the Scottish lords were poorer and had smaller households so they generally managed with just a single tower for themselves which was only slightly larger than each of the four standing at the corners of Bolton. The towers at Dean (p34), Cassillis (p28), Closeburn (p66), Sundrum (p56), and Caprington (p27) are all still habitable and have suffered alterations as a result, particularly the latter two which are nearly buried in later extensions. Threave (p116-9) is a well preserved ruin, Torthorwald (p84) and Glengarnock (p40) are much more damaged, and very little survives of the towers at Cruggleton (p96), Polnoon (p146), and Corsehill (p30). These towers originally stood alone except for outbuildings of wood in a palisaded court although a stone hall was added soon afterwards at Threave.

Caerlaverock Castle

The early towers generally have a lofty vaulted hall set over a vaulted cellar with a room or pair of rooms for the lord on top. At Threave and Torthorwald there were garrison mess rooms serving as kitchens between the hall and basement with the vault moved up to cover this intermediate storey. Often the only doorway was set high off the ground at hall level and was reached by timber steps from the ground. At Threave there is no upper vault and a fifth storey of sleeping space for retainers is provided over the lord's suite of two rooms. The tower at Portincross (p53) had only two storeys plus an attic but a pair of kitchens and the lord's suite were situated within a wing at one end. The halls in early towers tend to have a fireplace in an end wall (Threave is an exception) with windows in embrasures with seats in the adjacent parts of the sidewalls. The laird would have his table at this end while his retainers would sit in the cold and dark towards the other end adjacent to the entrance and staircase.

Two very different buildings also perhaps of this period are the triangular court with a hall-block and gatehouse at one end at Morton (p78), and a modest square tower at Sanquhar (p80) remaining from what may have been designed as a square court with corner towers. Remodellings of older gatehouse-keeps at Ardrossan (p21) and Dundonald (p36) have already been noted. The latter was a favoured seat of the first two Stewart Kings Robert II and III. At this time Bothwell (p125) finally gained a courtyard half the size of the intended original, the old keep being roughly patched up but superseded as the lord's residence by a square tower at the opposite end. The fragment remaining of this new principal tower has grooves of the beams of the drawbridge by which it was entered at second storey. Early in the 15th century an upper floor hall over cellars was built in front of it as part of a scheme including a chapel, apartments, and the fine round SE tower with its machicolated parapet. Crookston has impressive ruins of a massive and ambitiously planned tower house of c1400 with four corner towers providing space for many extra private rooms.

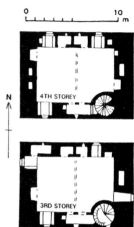

Comlongon Castle   *Plans of Law Castle*

The large mid 15th century towers at Covington (p130) and Comlongon (p66) are particularly massive. These towers had their entrances at ground level although at the slightly smaller contemporary tower at Mearns the entrance was at hall level. Comlongon is notable for having a complex series of mural chambers including two prisons, one of which is a dark dungeon below a guard room. The late 15th century Galloway towers of Cardoness (p90), Garlies (p102), and Rusko (p115) were similar to each other and each had a dark dungeon reached by a trap door from a less unpleasant prison above. The basements of these towers were divided into a smaller space used for storing drink and a larger space for foodstuffs. The same arrangement appears at Law (p47), which has a narrow kitchen divided off at one end of the hall, a feature also found at Comlongon. Other towers of this period are Barr (p122), Busby (p127), Castlemilk (p128), Craigneil (p31), Dalzell (p135), Kilbirnie (p43), Mochrum (p110), and Newark (p145), the last being quite small but having a gatehouse remaining from a vanished courtyard. Spedlins (p80) has been rebuilt above hall level, whilst little remains of the towers at Lamington (p142) and Wandel (p150).

In the 1440s a small court with round flanking towers fitted with gunloops was built around the tower at Threave. The subsequent siege by James II (p118) is the earliest recorded instance of guns being used either in defence or attack of a Scottish castle although bribery may have been more effective in inducing the garrison to surrender. There was a similar court either of this period or somewhat later around the demolished tower of Cathcart (p128). The court added at Dean (p34) in the 1460s contained a "Palace" or two storey hall block with a high tower at one end. The block with a round corner tower and a square stair wing at the opposite end at Dalquharran (p33) is of c1480 while there another much more ruined example at Strathavon (p149). Mid to late 15th century work at older castles includes the remodelling of the gatehouse and addition of retainers' apartments at Caerlaverock (p65), the gatehouse-keep with a projecting D-shaped tower containing a well at Sanquhar (p80), the extensions at Dunure (p37), the remodelling of the hall block at Craigie (p30), and a new hall block at Glengarnock (p40). The latter shares with the tower at Crookston the feature of round corner bartizans with machicolation slots. Orchardton (p112) has a very rare round tower house, while Ardstinchar (p22) has a fragment of a modest tower at one corner of a courtyard with several other square towers. Leven (p143) is an interesting instance of a tower of c1490 to which a wing only joined by one corner was added while the main block was under construction.

Craignethan is a courtyard castle of the 1530s with some unusual features as it was intended to be defended by and against firearms. A massive screen wall protects the weakest side and hidden in the bottom of the ditch in front of it was caponier or vaulted chamber allowing flanking fire without the risk of the flanker being exposed to cannonfire. The central tower house hidden behind the screen wall was mostly domestic in function. Cadzow may have been similar but is now very ruined.

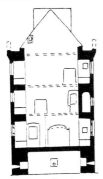

Law: Section

Craignethan Castle

Aumbry at Cardoness

Gilnockie Tower

Kilhenzie Castle showing round bartizans

Tower houses of the 16th century are very numerous. There was a general increase in prosperity and living standards, allowing and encouraging many lairds to build stone dwellings of some pretension for the first time coupled with a general sense of insecurity. The Stewart monarchs were dogged by a series of early deaths leading to the succession of minors, usually resulting in political termoil. There was interference from England in the form of invasions led by nobles and officials on behalf of the Crown and raids by lawless Border families. Cattle were the principal form of wealth in the Borders and were the main object of raids in all directions by families like the Armstrongs and Grahams who lived in and around the so-called Debateable Land. They could quickly raise hundreds of armed men on horseback and were too strong to be dislodged from what was supposed to be barren wasteland. In 1535 a statute ordered all men of substance in the borderland to build within two years stone barmkins with or without towers. Lesser men were encouraged to do likewise, an admission by the Crown that landowners needed to defend themselves. Two castles on islands in the Firth of Clyde, Ailsa Craig (p20) and Little Cumbrae (p48) were specifically built to control the ravages of pirates in the Irish Sea. Violent feuds between rival families were a way of life. In northern Ayrshire the Montgomeries fought the Cunninghames and in Dumfriesshire the Maxwells and Johnstones squabbled continuously as each in turn sought to be the most powerful and be recognised by the Crown with the office of Warden of the West March. In Carrick the Kennedys fought each other over former ecclesiastical estates while in Galloway they became embroiled in a series of disputes involving the Murrays, Hannays, the Dunbars and the Stewarts of Garlies, with the Agnews as hereditary sheriffs of Wigtown attempting to maintain the peace. Further round the coast the Browns of Carsluith and the M'Cullochs were uneasy neighbours, the former having remained Catholic whilst the latter supported the Reformation party. In the 1570s the Hamiltons supported the defeated Queen Mary and their castles in the Clyde Valley were captured by Regents acting for James VI.

Very few of the 16th century towers and mansions were intended to withstand cannonfire or a lengthy blockade. Hardly any of the towers have a water supply within them. However they were secure against raids by belligerent neighbours or cattle rustlers. The doorway would be closed by an iron yett sometimes with a thick oak door behind it, and all openings within easy reach of the ground would have bars or projecting grilles. Vaulted basements helped make towers fireproof and aided the structural stability of buildings with walls sometimes only a metre or so thick. Wide mouthed gunports appear in cellars and small round shot-holes are sometimes provided higher up. Otherwise towers could only be actively defended from the battlements. Parapets often overhang the walls on ornamental corbelling which is frequently the only decoration on a plain building with small openings and the rubble walls covered with a form of roughcast known as harling. Only cut stones would be left uncovered. Roundels or shallow open bartizans appear on the corners except for corner containing the staircase which sometimes had a gabled caphouse. Later in the 16th century the roofs are brought directly down onto the side walls either without wall-walks or with them only provided on the end walls, as at Craigcaffie (p95). Entrances are now usually at ground level although they are high off the ground at the towers of c1510-30 at Knockdolian (p47), Inverkip (p141), Little Cumbrae (p48), and Ailsa Craig (p20), while Hunterston (p42) has original entrances at both cellar and hall level.

Ayrshire towers tend to adhere to a standard layout of vaulted cellar, hall above, a two-room suite for the laird on the third storey, two bedrooms for his immediate family on the fourth storey, and servants' quarters in an attic within an open wall-walk. Newark (p51), Fairlie (p39), and Barr (p26) are examples, the latter two having subdivided basements. In smaller towers like Carleton (p28) and many of the towers near the Border like Gilnockie (p70), Bonshaw (p63), Lochhouse (p74), Stapleton (p82), and Hills (p102) the laird only had a single private room rather than a suite of two. Lochwood (p77) and Stranraer (p114) are early instances of the use of a small wing to contain the main staircase. Well preserved L-plan towers of c1550-1600 with the entrance at the foot of the stair in the wing are Abbot's (p86), Barholm (p88), Carsluith (p91), Drumcoltran (p97), Elshieshields (p69), Galdenoch (p101), Jerviston (p142), Kirkconnel (p105), Plunton (p111), and Pinwherry (p52).

Thomaston (p57) is a large low building with the wing extending over the former courtyard gateway. Hoddom (p71) is a large and massive L-plan building of the 1560s, later remodelled after siege damage. Baltersan (p25) has a main block long enough for the basement to be divided into a kitchen at the end furthest from the entrance, and separate cellars for food and drink with a passage connecting them all to the main staircase. This is a common layout in the late 16th and early 17th century. Here there is a second stair at the kitchen end as otherwise reaching the furthest bedroom from the main stair would be difficult. Park (p111), has a similar layout, and has a twin not far away with the added refinement of the main staircase being of the scale-and-platt type at Sorbie (p113). At Killochan (p44), and Dunskey (p99) the wing has a scale-and-platt stair just to the hall, then a smaller stair in a turret in the re-entrant angle takes over. Dunskey has a block adjoining the main tower which contains a long gallery like those found in Elizabethan mansions in England, while Killochan has a round tower on the outermost angle of the main block. Kirkhill (p46) has a similar layout on a smaller scale without the extra tower and with the stair in the re-entrant angle being corbelled out at hall level, a common layout in the late 16th century. The stair in a square stair projection in the re-entrant angle at Dunduff (p36) goes down to ground level and a kitchen is placed in the wing. Largest of all is the four storey L-planned mansion called Maclellan's Castle at Kircudbright (p107). It has space for a lobby between the hall and the chamber in the wing, and there is another chamber beyond the hall. Each level is connected by three staircases and there are numerous cellars and private rooms and a kitchen in the wing.

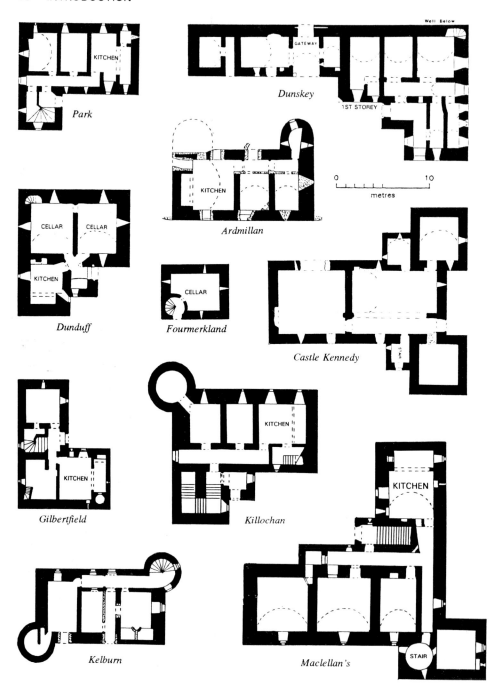

Plans of Castles of the Period 1570-1620

The mansion at Houston (p141) originally had four ranges around a central court like the royal palace at Linlithgow but only one much altered range now survives. Rowallan (p53) is also built around a small court although there were only two proper ranges, with the older tower house on a third side. The court lies upon a mound against which the cellars of one range are built and is entered by a gateway flanked by two small round turrets and approached by a long flight of steps.

Dargarvel (p135), Kelburn (p42), and Knock (p47) are so-called Z-plan castles of c1585-1600 with round towers at diagonally opposite corners of the main block. One tower contains a spiral staircase. The second tower at the more ruined castle of this type at Dalswinton (p136) may have been square. Ardmillan (p21) originally had two D-shaped towers projecting from either end of the entrance front. There was an increasing demand for external symmetry during the 17th century. Thus Castle Kennedy (p92) has both its square towers on the end facing the approach, and the long low unfortified building at Carscreugh (p91) has wings at either end of a side.

Round turrets called bartizans corbelled out near the eaves and containing closets opening off the topmost storey or attic are common in the period 1560-1620. The bartizans are often furnished with tiny shotholes for handguns. Two of them set at diagonally opposite corners appear on the small nearly square towers of Isle (p72) and Fourmerkland (p69) in Dumfriesshire. Amisfield (p60) is an instance of an only slightly larger tower of c1530 rebuilt c1600 with bartizans on three corners and a two storied caphouse over the stair which projects from the fourth corner from the hall level upwards. A tiny garret opening off these is squeezed onto the adjacent gable. At Elshieshields there is a stance for a warning beacon fire in the same position and a number of towers near the Border were formerly furnished with them. From the mid 16th century onwards it was common for stones carved with arms, initials, and dates to be placed over the doorway. Many of these survive and fix the time of construction or alteration although in some cases they were put up to commemorate important family events. Openings in this period are sometimes embellished with a roll moulding while gables are finished with crow-steps rising to a central chimney. The hall or main living room now often has a fireplace along one side heating the whole room better than a fire just at the laird's table end, and necessitating a freestanding chimney which was easier to provide when there was no wall-walk for such a stack to block.

Date stone at Fourmerkland Tower

Killochan Castle

Cassillis (p28) and Frenchland (p69) are instances of older towers which were remodelled in the early 17th century with the addition of a stair wing and new roofs replacing former open wall-walks. A new mansion of the 1590s with a semi-symmetrical layout and big windows with pedimental heads joins the older tower and gatehouse at Newark (p145). There are segmental window pediments in the splendid ashlar faced facade of the range added in the 1630s at Caerlaverock (p65). Loudon (p49) and Kilbirnie (p43) are instances of spacious wings of the same period being added to older tower houses. At Sanquhar (p80) a thinly walled outer court containing outbuildings was added. As the 17th century wore on castellated features like turrets and gunports were done away with altogether as at Baldoon (p86), and Barscobe (p88), which are essentially large farmhouses lacking any means of defence although the latter has vaulted cellars. Similar to them are the series of T-plan houses of c1600-30 in Ayrshire with a centrally placed wing containing the staircase, as at Monk (p50), Brunston (p27), Crosbie (p31), and Auchans (p23). The last was later extended by a wing with various other turrets. Clonbeith (p29) is shorter and had a stair corbelled out over a centrally placed entrance. All of these are thinly walled and lack gunports but a single shot-hole covers the entrance from the slight projection which contains the stair at Blackhall (p123).

The internal walls of castles at all periods would be plastered and either painted with biblical or heroic scenes or covered with hangings with similar themes. Carpets only became common at the end of the 16th century. If it lay on top of a vault the hall floor might be of polished stone slabs but other floors were usually of wooden planks laid on heavy beams and sometimes covered in straw or rushes renewed occasionally. Early windows were closed with wooden shutters but by the 16th century glass was more common and a contract of 1568 survives for the making of windows for the Earl of Eglinton's country seats of Eglinton, Ardrossan, Polnoon, Little Cumbrae, and his town houses at Glasgow and Irvine. The sash windows and other openable glass windows usually found in the larger openings of still inhabited towers are insertions of the 18th century and later. Latrines with open drains are less common in late buildings when chamber pots were fashionable.

Crosbie Castle

The range of the 1630s at Caerlaverock   *Blackhall under restoration*

Even as late as the 17th century there was often a lack of personal privacy in Scottish castles. Many children or servants might have to share not only the same room but one large bed. Only the laird and his immediate adult relations would have individual rooms allocated to them. Others might sleep in the hall or perhaps in the kitchen or anywhere where they could make themselves comfortable. Even lairds sometimes had a servant or bodyguard also sleeping in their room although partitions and hangings, and the curtains of four poster 16th and 17th century beds, would give a little privacy. Normally the number of persons in permanent residence in a tower house, especially the smaller ones, might be less than a dozen.

The outbreak of war between King Charles I and the Covenanters saw the capture and destruction of the Maxwell castles of Caerlaverock and Threave by the Covenant forces in 1640. Few of the other castles saw any action in that period, although a description of Ardmillan Castle written in 1687 suggests that unrest in some areas continued throughout much of Charles II's reign. By the time of the Union with England in 1707 there was peace and already a number of lairds had moved out of dark and cramped old towers into more modern mansions nearby. By the 19th century the majority of the castles had fallen into ruin but Buittle Place and Penkhill were then restored, and Dean was repaired in the 1930s. Since 1970 Aiket, Gilnockie, Law, Leven, Rusco, and Spedlins have been restored from ruin and Crawfurdland, Park, and Waygateshaw have been refurbished. Plans are afoot for the restoration of several others such as Baltersan, Fairlie, and Greenan.

GAZETTEER OF CASTLES IN AYRSHIRE

AIKET NS 388488

The original tower by a bend of the Glazer Burn was built for Alexander Cunninghame and Janet Kennedy c1479. It bears modern stones on dormer pediments with their initials and those of the couple who restored the building c1980. It was probably a later Alexander Cunninghame who was involved in the murder of the Montgomery Earl of Cunninghame in 1586 and was afterwards shot near his home, who extended the building to the SW, giving it a total length of 15.3m. The castle was later remodelled as a tall but plain three storey house with a gabled doorway and a scale-and-platt staircase in the middle, and passed from the Cunninghames in the early 18th century. The restorers rebuilt most of the walls from the second storey upwards and changed the roof-line, which had been altered to a single level, back to how it was c1600 with the original tower rising one stage above the three storey wing with a round bartizan on the NW corner. They have also re-instated a 16th or 17th century round stair turret at the back which had been removed.

AILSA CRAIG NX 023995

Ailsa Craig is a precipitous rock 338m high lying in the Firth of Clyde 16km west of Girvan. Perched 90m above the sea beside the path from the only landing place to the summit is a ruined tower with traces of a tiny barmkin on the north side. It is thought to have been built in the early 16th century to prevent pirates occupying the rock. The tower measures just 6.7m by 5.0 and has a doorway high up in the east wall. This gives access to a vaulted room with three loops and to a mural stair running up to a spiral stair in the SE corner. The room above has a fireplace with an oven in the west wall and a mural room over the entrance. A trap-door formed the only access to a dark vaulted basement. There may have been another storey and perhaps corner turrets.

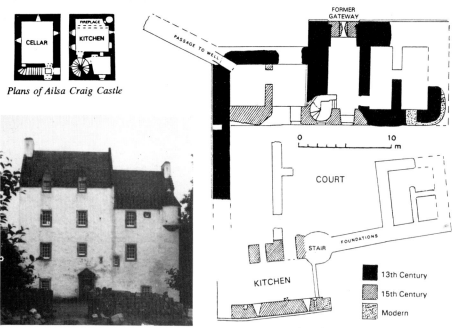

Plans of Ailsa Craig Castle

Aiket Castle

Plan of Ardrossan Castle

ARDMILLAN NX 169945

Ardmillan formed part of the Kennedy barony of Bargany and Ardstinchar in 1476 but later passed to a junior branch of the family. The house which remained occupied until a 20th century accidental fire and now lies derelict is assumed to have been built by Thomas Kennedy who tried unsuccessfully to be made tutor to the new laird of the barony after Gilbert, the previous incumbent, was murdered in 1601. James Crawford of Baidland acquired Ardmillan in 1658 by marrying Marion Kennedy. Two decades later Abercrummie described the castle as having a dry moat, of which there is now no sign, crossed by a movable bridge. The courtyard he mentions has been partly filled up with later extensions. The castle originally comprised a block 15m long by 7.4m wide with the usual basement layout of a kitchen with a fireplace in the north end wall (now hidden by panelling) and two cellars connected by a passage on the east side. Above was the hall, then a pair of bedrooms, and finally an attic. There are tiny bartizans on the west corners and there were round turrets with square caphouses projecting from either end of the east front. Only the south turret survives on a somewhat altered state, the caphouse gable now being set back behind the curved walling below, instead of carried forward on corbelled courses, and a staircase probably having been removed. The upper parts of the other turret were left supported on girders as a result of 19th century alterations and it has now gone altogether.

ARDROSSAN A.M. NS 233424

The Barclays may have had a castle on the ridge above the modern port in the 12th century. The Ardrossans may have been descended from them and had a stone-built court and gatehouse here by the time of Wallace, who is said to have dismantled it. The building was restored and passed to Sir John Montgomerie who fought at Otterburn in 1388 and Homildon Hill in 1402. His son was created Lord Montgomerie c1445, and his grandson became 1st Earl of Eglinton in 1508. The family sought refuge here in 1528 when their chief seat at Eglinton was sacked by the Cunninghames, but the building was subsequently little used. It was a ruin by 1689 and the then Earl plundered it for materials c1748 for walling in a new park nearby.

Ardrossan Castle

Walls up to 1.9m thick enclose a square court with steep slopes to the east and south but level ground on the other sides where there was a ditch, now nearly filled in. There are traces of buildings of later date on all four sides. The base of a spiral stair adjoins a vaulted kitchen on the south side. A low pointed doorway in the NW corner leads to a long passage to a well in the middle of the former ditch. Filling much of the north side is what was originally a gatehouse 15.5m long by 11.0 wide. At courtyard level were three compartments of which the westernmost was the entrance passage. A pair of vaulted cellars called the Vallance Lardner lie below the other two. The building shows clear signs of dismantling c1300 and later rebuilding with sandstone instead of the original limestone. The outer entrance to the passage was then blocked and a narrower doorway with an adjacent spiral stair replaced the inner end of the passage. Little remains of the upper rooms except one jamb of a fine fireplace at third storey level in the north wall but the building seems to have always contained the hall and principal private apartment above, although further chambers opening off them or the staircase were later added in the NW corner of the courtyard. The courtyard was entered from the east by c1500 but there may have been an interim entrance in the north wall beside the old gatehouse before the chambers were built there. The only certain evidence of 16th century alterations is a double splayed gunport inserted in the blocking of the outer arch of the former entrance passage.

ARDSTINCHAR   NX 086824

This castle on a crag above the lowest bridgehead of the River Stinchar is said to have been built in the mid 15th century by Hugh Kennedy, a younger son of Lord Kennedy of Dunure, who was destined for the church but achieved fame and fortune serving Charles VII of France before returning to purchase this estate. In nearby Ballantrae kirkyard is the fine tomb of Hugh's descendant Gilbert, 16th baron of Bargany and Ardstinchar who was killed at Maybole in 1601 in a fight against the superior forces of his cousin the Earl of Cassillis. A quarrel originating over custody of the former lands of Crossraguel Abbey had been further nurtured by disputes over possession of the other Kennedy estates of Brunston and Newark and the Earl had recently managed to avoid an attempted kidnapping by the lairds of Drummurchie and Bennan. The castle probably fell into decay soon after as the Bargany barons became impoverished.

Ardstinchar Castle

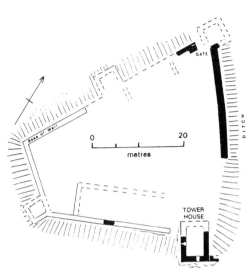

Plan of Ardstinchar Castle

Auchans Castle

The castle consists of a wedge shaped court with footings of a wall about 1m thick overlooking the south, west, and NW slopes. More survives of the 1.5m thick wall above a ditch dividing the site from higher ground to the east. There are traces of a square tower at the north corner with the drawbar slot of a gateway beside it, and signs of other square towers in the middle of the NW side and at the SW corner and there seems to have been a large hall on the south side. East of this is the principal tower containing the private rooms. It stands on a crag and had at least four storeys with vaults set at difference axes over the second and fourth. The two topmost rooms had fireplaces in the SW side wall. The whole of the north end has fallen and only a fragment remains of a later wing to the east.

AUCHANS   NS 355346

The Wallaces of Dundonald acquired the neighbouring estate of Auchans in 1527 and built a house 17m long by 6.8m wide c1600. A spiral stair in a round turret in the middle of the south side connected the hall and private room on the second storey with three vaulted cellars below, and bedrooms and attics above. A wing 11m long added at the west end of the north side by Sir William Cochrane after his purchase of Auchans in 1638 contained four storeys and an attic. It was not intended to be defensible, the unvaulted lowest room having windows without bars or grilles. A square staircase turret added within the re-entrant angle formerly bore the date 1644. Cochrane was made a baron by Charles I, and in 1669 was created Earl of Dundonald. About that time the wing was extended by a further 10m to the north with a round turret provided at the NW corner, and another on the east side containing a third spiral stair. The extension contained three storeys of fine rooms over a vaulted kitchen which is now full of rubble. The later Earls of Dundonald lived at Gwyrch Castle in North Wales, Auchans being then held by the Earls of Eglinton. It was granted as a jointure house to Suzanna Kennedy when she married the 9th Earl and she lived out her old age there. By the 19th century Auchans contained only workmen's families and it later fell into ruin. The shell remains except for the later wing NE corner.

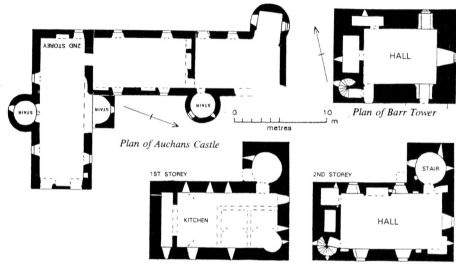

Plan of Auchans Castle

Plan of Barr Tower

Plans of Baltersan Castle

AUCHENCLOIGH   NS 495166

A few fallen fragments of a modestly sized 16th century tower lie on a slight rise above a burn east of Auchencloigh farmhouse, 5km SSW of Ochiltree.

AUCHENHARVIE   NS 363443

This early 16th century tower was later abandoned by the Cunninghames in favour of Seabank House at Stevenson. It measured 11m by 8.8m over walls 2m thick now mostly robbed of dressed stone and had vaults over both the basement and hall. The entrance and lower stair were in the destroyed east side. A spiral stair in the NW corner then led up to the wall-walk which had a parapet and roundels on continuous corbel coursing. The tower now stands oddly isolated in the midst of a quarry pit.

AUCHINLECK   NS 500232

Nothing remains of the tower of the Auchinleck family, lairds from 1292 until c1500, and only minor overgrown fragments survive the Boswells' early 17th century L-plan house which had a high stair turret with a gabled caphouse in the re-entrant angle. It lies near the junction of the Dippon Burn and Lugar Water and was abandoned after a new mansion visited by Dr Johnson in 1773 was built for his friend James Boswell. This in turn was replaced by an early 19th century mansion, also now neglected.

AYR   NS 333223

William the Lion's motte of c1197 stood in the angle between the south bank of the River Ayr and the sea. Alexander III is thought to have rebuilt the castle in stone on a plan reported as a triangle with round corner towers. It is said to have been occupied by Bruce in his capacity as sheriff in 1302, although he is claimed to have destroyed it only three years before. It had certainly been destroyed by the time of his death. In the 1650s Cromwell built a hexagonal 12 acre fort on the site. The old church of St John thus enclosed then became an armoury. Parts of the outer walls including one sentry box perched on bold corbelling like those at Dumbarton and Edinburgh survive.

BALTERSAN NS 282087

In 1530 Egidia Blair, Lady Row, died in her house of Baltersan, the estate being held on a lease from Crossraguel Abbey. The present building was built for David Kennedy of Penyglen who obtained the estate in 1574 from Allan Stewart, Commendator of the abbey. Until recently the building was a solitary ruin in a field, the gardens, orchards, parks, and woods mentioned by Abercrummie in 1679 having all gone. The castle is one of the finer tower houses of its period in Ayrshire with superior features like roll moulded inner arches for all the windows. It is an L-planned structure 15.4m long by 8.4m wide with the wing containing a wide spiral stair from the entrance to the hall and the laird's suite on the third storey. A narrow stair in a square turret over the re-entrant angle then led up to the fourth storey rooms, including one in the wing with an oriel upon three corbels, and the attics in the roof. On the NW and SE corners are round bartizans with machicolation slots and pistol loops. The original vaults and dividing walls of the kitchen and wine and food cellars have been destroyed. The west end wall is thickened to contain the kitchen fireplace flue which at hall level is flanked by a closet and a secondary spiral stair giving direct access to the laird's private room.

BARGANY NS 244003

Abercrummy describes the former chief seat of the Kennedy barons of Bargany and Ardstinchar on the south bank of the Water of Girvan as a large tower house in the middle of a quadrangular court with four storey towers at three of the corners. It provided materials for building the mansion of the Dalrymple Earls of Stair closeby to the south which bears the initials H.B. and the year 1681 on a dormer window of the oldest part.

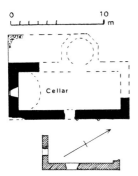

Plan of Brunston Castle

Baltersan Castle

Blair Castle

BARR NS 502365

George Wishart and John Knox are said to have preached in 1545 and 1556 respectively in this tower of c1500 built by the Lockharts in the middle of the town of Galston. The four storey tower is now covered with a modern hipped roof and is only used for meetings. It measures 13.4m by 10m with walls 2.1m thick except for the even thicker west wall containing mural chambers opening off the spiral stair in the SW corner. It seems that the original entrance was at hall level beside this stair and the present entrance below it is a later insertion. At the summit are two alternating rows of corbels for the destroyed parapets and roundels.

BLAIR NS 305480

The modern stone over the entrance with the initials B.B. and the date 1203 commemorate the fact that the Blairs have had a seat here above a bend of the Bombo Burn from early times. The core of the house is a tower house 10.8m long by 8m wide, probably 15th century although no ancient features remain within it. It was later extended to the east and then the building was remodelled as a gabled house with a slim new turret containing the entrance above which is a stone, perhaps reset, with the date 1617 and the initials of Bryce Blair and Annabel Wallace of Craigie. Further above are 17th century stones in memory of 13th century owners Roger de Blair and Marie Mair. A long three storey south wing has dormer pediments with the date 1668 and the initials of William Blair and Lady Margaret Hamilton. The same date appears over a new entrance in a turret added beside the older one in the re-entrant angle. In 1893 the building was widened northwards to provide better access between the various rooms and the four storey east wing probably of c1680-1700 mostly rebuilt.

BRISBANE NS 209622

A four storey mansion built by the Shaws of Greenock and dated 1634 once stood in the glen of the Noddsdale Water 3km NNE of Largs. In 1650 Robert Kelso repurchased the estate which had belonged to the Kelsos from the 13th century until 1624 and was then called Kelsoland. The name was changed after it was sold to James Brisbane of Bishoptoun in 1671. He added wings attached to the main block by means of low curving corridors. The main facade was symmetrical with three tiers of windows on either side of the entrance, and smaller gables on either side of a large central one.

BRUNSTON   NS 261012

By the Water of Girvan 1km west of Dailly is a very ruined and overgrown early 17th century house 13m long by 6m wide which once had a polygonal stair turret with a square caphouse in the middle of the now destroyed NW side. Most of the vaulted basement is filled with earth and rubble. One high fragment shows that there was a third storey over the hall and private room end to end on the second storey. An older house here was occupied by "Black Bessie" Kennedy after the death of her third husband William, Baillie of Carrick. Her relatives Lord Bargany and the Earl of Cassillis had a long and bitter quarrel over possession of Bessie and her lands (see Ardstinchar).

BUSBIE   NS 397390

A ruined four storey tower built c1600 by the Mowats above the west bank of Carmel Water behind the houses of Knockentiber 3km WNW of Kilmarnock was demolished in the 1950s. Old drawings show that it was about 11.3m long by 7.2m wide and had two cellars with widely splayed gunloops. One corner had a gabled caphouse over the spiral stair and the others had round bartizans with rope mouldings at top and bottom.

CAMREGAN   NX 206988

There are slight remains of a tower on a hillside above a stream 3km NE of Girvan.

CAPRINGTON   NS 407363

This castle was remodelled by Sir William Cunninghame c1800 with large new windows, mock battlements, turrets, and additions masking the rocky base. The tower 14.6m long by 10m wide with walls well over 2m thick forming the nucleus may date back to the time of Sir Duncan Wallace of Sundrum who obtained the estate in 1385. The Cunninghames provided the tower with new battlements with corner roundels and a stair wing c1500, and then later added a large gabled block providing many extra rooms and more than doubling the size of the building.

Caprington Castle   *Brunston
Castle*

Carleton Castle

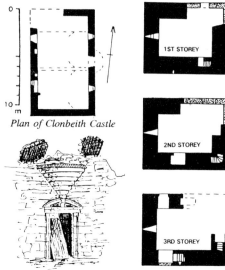

Plan of Clonbeith Castle

Clonbeith Castle

Plans of Carleton Castle

CARLETON NX 134895

The Cathcarts' 5m high motte with a summit 20m across and their ruined tower of c1500 lie on either side of a lane and burn high above the sea near Lendalfoot. The tower once had a small barmkin on a promontory and measures 9.3m by 7.5m. The destroyed NE corner contained the entrance and probably a stair connecting at least the cellar, the hall, and the storey between which was perhaps a kitchen. A crudely made service stair in the SE corner connects the cellar and hall and a mural stair from a hall side window led to the private room and wall-walk within which was an attic.

CARNELL NS 466322

The castle may have been originally built by Adam Wallace who died in 1510.In the kitchen is a stone bearing the date 1569 and the Wallace and Mure arms originally set over the entrance. Hew Wallace had then recently been accused of complicity in Lord Darnley's murder. Carnell passed to the Cathcarts in the 17th century but was later regained by the Wallaces and held by them until the mid 20th century.

CASSILLIS NS 341128

The large tower house 18m long by 12m wide with walls 3.6m thick above the south bank of the Doon was built for Sir John Kennedy who married the heiress of Sir Neil Montgomery c1370, a charter of the lands then being obtained from David II. Sir John's grandson was made Earl of Cassillis in 1502 and the castle remained the chief seat of the earldom until 1762 when Sir Thomas Kennedy of Culzean became 9th Earl and chose to remain at his original seat. Now that Culzean has been handed over to the National Trust the 18th Earl, also 7th Marquis of Ailsa, a title granted in 1831, lives back at Cassillis. In the 16th century the scholar George Buchanan wrote his Somnium at the castle while acting as tutor to the young Earl Gilbert. In the 17th century the tower was remodelled with a wide circular staircase in a new wing, and a new top storey upon continuous corbelled coursing with conical roofed bartizans and a short section of balustraded parapet. Adjoining the wing are the considerable additions made by Sir Archibald Kennedy shortly before his death in 1832.

Cassillis Castle

Cessnock Castle

CESSNOCK   NS 511355

The tower at the southern corner of a mansion built around a small court set high above the junction of Burn Annie and a tributary near Galston was probably built c1520 for John Campbell, a cadet of the Campbells of Loudon. The vaulted basement has a doorway but only communicated with the hall by means of a hatch, the main entrance and start of the staircase being at that level. The two upper storeys have rooms in a thick end wall above the ravine. The battlements have been removed and a wider new attic substituted for the original within the wall-walk. The west corner is cambered off up to the level of the hall ceiling and then is corbelled out to a square. A roof-mark shows that the now open west corner of the court once had a building. Sir George Campbell is said to have begun the later extensions between 1578 and 1597 but much of them as they now stand was built by his grandson Sir Hew, his initials and the year 1666 appearing on one of two stair turrets projecting into the court, while the NW range has the dates 1670 and 1675 and a plaster ceiling inside is dated 1680. Sir Hew supported the Covenant and he was imprisoned and forfeited by James II in 1685 but was restored after William III's accession in 1688. His son George added the other turret stair in the 1690s, and was succeeded by his son-in-law Sir James Hume, who assumed the Campbell surname. Considerable repairs and alterations were carried out for the Duke of Portland in the 19th century.

CLONBEITH   NS 395442

The basement of a thinly walled mansion of the Cunninghames lie in a farmyard. The east front was symmetrical and had windows either side of a doorway dated 1607 above which a round staircase turret was corbelled out. The cellars once had vaults. The hall was reached by a stair at the north end reached presumably from the doorway by a short passage past the northern cellar. The windows were fitted with bars. Clonbeith was sold in 1717 to the Earl of Eglinton.

CLONCAIRD   NS 359075

Incorporated in Henry Richie's mansión of 1814 on the east bank of the Water of Girvan is the much altered 16th century tower of Water Mure. He was involved in the murder of Sir Thomas Kennedy of Culzean in 1602.

CORSEHILL   NS 416456

Between the A735 and the railway north of Stewarton are two fragments of a massive early Cunninghame tower measuring about 13m by 12m over walls 2.4m thick above the basement vault and 3m thick below. The only surviving features are a fireplace high up and part of the well of a stair near the NE corner.

CRAIGIE   NS 408317

John Wallace of Riccarton obtained Craigie c1371 by marrying a Lindsay heiress. His successors lived there until the 17th century after which it became ruinous. The original 13th hall house of the Lindsays was 11m wide over walls 1.8m thick and contained an undivided hall over a low unvaulted basement. In the 15th century the walls were thickened internally, doubled in height to provide space for a private suite of rooms over the hall, and extended at either end to a new overall length of about 28m. The original battlements and holes draining the wall-walk are visible in the outer wall faces just below the windows of the heightened hall which then measured 14m by 6.5m and was ashlar faced with three bays of finely ribbed vaulting. One of the windows was later blocked to accommodate a fireplace and the flue of a kitchen fireplace ascending from below. On either side of the hall house were unconnected courts, that on the north having remains of a series of cellars.

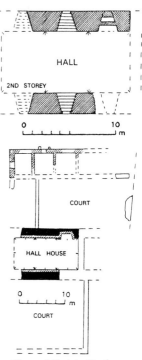

Plans of Craigie Castle

Hall at Craigie Castle

Plan of Corsehill Castle

Crawfurdland Castle

Craigneil Castle

CRAIGNEIL   NX 147854

This 15th century tower stands dramatically on a hill south of the River Stinchar opposite Colmonell. Quarrying up to the base has caused the collapse of the north corner but the rest stands four storeys high with remains of a vault over the lofty third storey hall. There was a spiral stair in the south corner and a ragged hole with a drawbar hole marks the entrance beside it. The thick adjoining end wall contains small chambers. The tower measures 12.6m by 9.3m with walls averaging 1.9m thick.

CRAWFURDLAND   NS 456408

On the SW side of the large 19th century mansion is the Crawfurd's mid 16th century tower which was restored in the 1980s. It has three storeys plus an attic within a parapet on continuous corbelled coursing with corner roundels. There is a square gabled caphouse over the staircase in the north corner. One widely splayed gunport survives in the vaulted cellar.

CROSBIE   NS 217500

Crosbie belonged to a cadet branch of the Crawfurds of Loudon from the 13th century until the 20th. The present house is a 17th century structure restored in the late 19th century, later used as a Youth Hostel, and now in the centre of a caravan park. the long rectangular block has three rooms on each of three storeys with attics above. Linking them is a stair in a turret in the middle of the south side. See photo p18.

Dalquharran Castle

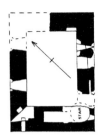

Plan of Craigneil Castle

CROSSRAGUEL A.M. NS 275084

The tower at the east end of the 14th century Abbot's House at Crossraguel Abbey was added c1530 by Abbot William Kennedy either as a residence for himself or for his young nephew the 3rd Earl of Cassillis of whom he was guardian for 11 years. It measures 8.7m by 8.4m and has walls from 1.8m to 2.1m thick. It was entered by a lobby contained in a turret near the west corner. The basement was vaulted and has loops with roundels at the foot. It has its own entrance and a service stair to the hall. The private room and bedroom are also connected by a stair, but the staircase from the hall to the private room must have been within the destroyed north corner.

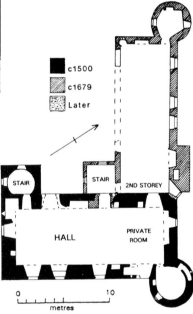

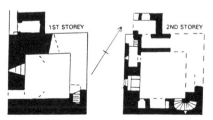

Plans of the tower at Crossraguel Abbey

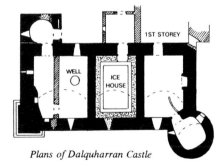

Plans of Dalquharran Castle

CULZEAN   A.M.   NS 233103

Robert Adam's masterpiece for the 10th Earl of Cassillis overlooking the Firth of Clyde incorporates some masonry of a gabled L-plan tower built by Sir Thomas Kennedy. He was laird of Culzean from 1549 until he was murdered on the sands at Ayr in 1602 in retribution for the recent killing of his kinsman the laird of Bargany during a feud originally started over possession of other Kennedy estates. The Picture Room represents the hall of the tower although all its features are of c1780. When Sir Thomas Kennedy became 9th Earl in 1762 he began some additions and improvements but these seem to have been mostly swept away to make room for his brother David's mansion. At the coronation of William IV in 1831 the new King made his friend the 12th Earl Marquis of Ailsa. In 1945 the 5th Marquis gave the castle and estate to the Scottish National Trust by whom the building has been comprehensively restored both inside and out. The family then transferred back to the original seat of the earldom, Cassillis Castle.

DALBLAIR   NS 647192

A 5m high fragment of the 1.9m thick north wall with jambs of two hall windows is all that remains of the 16th century Cunninghame stronghold of Dalblair or Kyle. The tower measured about 14m by 9m and occupied half the width of the neck of a triangular promontory above the junction of Glenmuir Water and Guelt Water.

DALQUHARRAN   NS 273019

Edward Bruce, Earl of Carrick, gave Dalquharran to Crossraguel Abbey in 1324. By the late 15th century it was in the hands of the Kennedys, presumably as tenants of the Abbey. They built a "palace" or self contained hall block on the north bank of the Water of Girvan, almost opposite the modern village of Dailly. In 1536 the castle was held by John Kennedy of Culzean but it was later acquired by the Kennedys of Girvan Mains, a junior branch of the Cassillis branch of the family. The ruinous long three storey NW wing has a round tower with pentagonal rooms on the north corner. The initials of Sir James and Dame Margaret Kennedy appear on a fireplace in a chimney breast projection by the junction with the older work. In the re-entrant angle is a turret dated 1679 with rusticated quoins. It contained a scale-and-platt staircase. The pair of fine Baroque gateposts nearby to the west must be of the same period. Not long afterwards Dalquharran, Girvan Mains, and Dunure were purchased by Sir Thomas Kennedy of Kirkhill, Lord Provost of Edinburgh. The castle at Dalquharran was left to decay after a new mansion, now also ruined, was built to the NW in 1790.

The original hall block is a building of some interest, retaining many of its features despite having been altered and ruined. It seems that there was a pause in construction after the three vaulted cellars each with direct access from the outside had been built. When the hall 10.5m long and 6m wide and the private chamber partitioned off at the north end were added they were given slightly thicker walling than below, and a square turret containing the entrance and staircase was added in front of the hall doorway. The round tower at the diagonally opposite corner may have been planned from the start. The southern corner has thinly projecting buttressing not carried above the level of the vaults. In the 17th century the southern cellar was subdivided whilst in the 18th century the middle cellar was brick lined to convert it into an ice-house. The hall fireplace was reduced in width when the stair turret of 1679 was added. The private room has a fireplace and several lockers one of which is a finely decorated niche containing the Kennedy arms. A service stair once led down to the middle cellar. There was a third storey divided probably into three bedrooms with a fourth in the round tower. At the top was a parapet carried all round at a constant height on corbels carrying lintels with ogival arches cut into them.

DEAN   A.M.*   NS 437394

Dean Castle lies in a public park NW of the centre of Kilmarnock. Robert I granted the estate to the Boyds in 1316 and by the end of that century they had built a large tower house 16m long by 11m wide with walls up to 2.7m thick above a wide battered plinth. The vaulted basement has an entrance at the north end with a service stair leading off it and is divided by a later crosswall. The southern cellar has an inserted fireplace using a former latrine shoot as a flue. The hall is a lofty barrel vaulted room with a staircase leading to a window embrasure high up at the northern end which served as a musicians gallery. Below this window is the original main entrance which in the 17th century was replaced by another doorway created out of one of two window embrasures near the south end. This is reached by a new open stair against the east wall. The private room above has an oratory in the thickness of the north wall. The fourth storey lies within the wall-walk and has a caphouse over the staircase. Finally there is an attic within the roof itself.

In 1466 the Boyds got possession of the young James III and ruled Scotland in his name. In 1467 Thomas, eldest son of Robert, Lord Boyd. married the King's sister Mary and was created Earl of Arran. Like most regents, especially those not originally of the highest rank, the Boyds soon became unpopular and had to flee to Denmark. During this short period Dean castle was improved to match their new status. A courtyard was built east of the tower with a suite of apartments on the south side ending on the east with a lofty tower with a parapet boldly corbelled out. The apartments, known as The Palace comprise a hall and private chamber end-to-end above a kitchen and two cellars. A second private room is contained in the tower and there are bedrooms above. An addition containing a new staircase and entrance bears the monogram of James Boyd, who died in 1654, and his wife Dame Catherine Creyk.

James was succeeded by William, created Earl of Kilmarnock in 1661. The Palace was accidentally burnt out in 1735 and the 4th Earl was executed for his part in the 1745 Jacobite rebellion. The castle was sold and passed in 1828 to Lord Howard de Walden. The 8th Lord Howard de Walden restored the ruin, adding a roofed wall-walk on the east curtain wall and a gatehouse on the north side. The 9th Lord gave the castle to the town in 1975 and it now serves as a museum.

DRONGAN   NS 450178

The last remains of a 15th century tower by the Water of Coyle have been removed.

Dean Castle

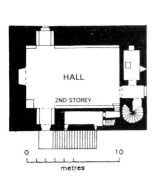

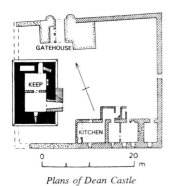

Plans of Dean Castle

Dean Castle

Dundonald Castle from the east

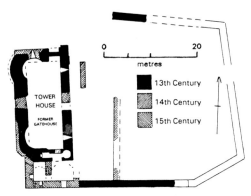

Dundonald Castle   Plan of Dundonald Castle

DUNDONALD   A.M.   NS 364345

Walter Fitz-Alan had a wooden castle upon this hill-top in the 12th century. His great-great grandson James the High Steward, one of the leading nobles of the 1290s built a wall 1.6m thick around three sides of a court roughly 24m square entered through a gatehouse occupying most of the west side. The wall is mostly reduced to footings except for a substantial section on the south side, where a 15th century wall of uncertain purpose extending far into the court meets it. The gatehouse may never have been completed and in any case was dismantled during Robert Bruce's reign. Robert II had it rebuilt as a huge tower house in the 1370s and frequently resided here. The castle was later held by the Boyds and then the Wallaces and was presumably left to decay after the latter developed a more up-to-date mansion nearby at Auchans.

The gatehouse as remodelled as a tower house with the original entrance passage blocked up and the original shallow pair of rounded outer faces to the flanking towers almost obliterated is now a rectangle of 24m by 12m. The lowest level became a dark storage area perhaps divided by timber partitions. The storey above became common hall probably with a private room divided off at the north end furthest from the new entrance made in the south wall. Above was a pointed vaulted third storey also probably divided into two chambers, the largest of which has a fireplace in the west wall. This was presumably the royal suite, although the rooms were very dark. Above the vault was the great hall, an impressive apartment covered with a point vault with quadripartite ribs of purely decorative purpose forming two square bays with a service area at the south end. This hall was reached by a spiral stair in the SE corner. A 15th century addition at the south end containing a vaulted prison and bakehouse side by side with private rooms above, is now very ruinous.

DUNDUFF   NS 272164

High above the sea NW of Dunure are the two lowest storeys of an L-plan tower house built by the Kennedys c1580-1600. The walls are broken off fairly evenly all round suggesting that the building was either never finished or has been partly dismantled for materials. The main block 12.4m long by 8.2m wide with walls 1.5m thick contains separate cellars for food and wine, the latter having a service stair to the hall above. The wing contained a small kitchen with a private room above. A passage between the private room and hall allows the latter to be entered at its NW end from a stair in a turret in the re-entrant angle with the entrance at its foot.

Dunduff Castle

DUNLOP NS 428493

Above the hall doorway of the house of 1834 is a stone bearing the dates 1599 and 1603 which came from an older house on this site called Hunthall.

DUNURE A.M. NS 253158

Dunure was the first castle built by the Kennedy family and remained an important seat of the chief after Cassillis became the main seat. Clearance and investigation of the ruins in the 1980s has prompted the suggestion that the original tower 14.7m long by 9.3m wide with walls 1.5m thick dates back to the late 13th century. With the advancement of the family fortunes in the 15th century the tower was rebuilt and extended both to seaward and landward with blocks containing many extra chambers. The portion at the extreme end of the cliff-top site stands three storeys high complete with the corbels for the former parapet although not enough remains internally for the arrangements to be understood. Not much of the tower now stands above the level of the basement which was divided by a passage linking the two parts and having pairs of small cellars on either side.

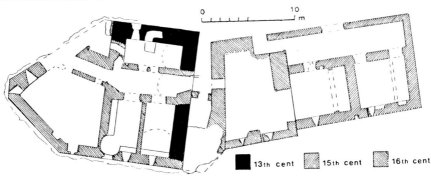

Plan of Dunure Castle

Old print of Dunure Castle

Gilbert Kennedy, 4th Earl of Cassillis obtained lands from Glenluce Abbey in Galloway by having a monk forge the necessary signatures. The monk was silenced by a hired killer who in turn was hung after being found guilty of theft by the Kennedys. In 1565 the Earl confined Allan Stewart, Commendator of Crossraguel Abbey, in Dunure Castle and tortured him into renouncing a claim to the abbey lands. Lord Bargany coveted the abbey lands himself and had the castle stormed one morning by a force of men concealed in a chapel just outside the main gate. The Earl then besieged the castle and his men also used the chapel for cover, this time for mining operations against the wall until the chapel roof was smashed by large stones dropped from the battlements. Bargany then appeared with a strong force and the Commendator was removed to Ayr and the lands redistributed by negotiation, the Commendator being pensioned off. The Earl presumably dismantled the chapel as soon as he got the castle back and the present block containing several private rooms over a pair of kitchens must have been erected soon afterwards.

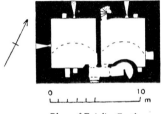

Plan of Fairlie Castle

Fairlie Castle

EGLINTON NS 323422

This was the chief seat of the Montgomeries, created Earls of Eglinton in 1508. It must have been fortified in stone at an early date and was presumably repaired and extended after being burnt in 1528 during their feud with the Cunninghames. It does not appear that there are any remains of it within the new mansion built in 1798 by Hugh, the 12th Earl. The direct male line died out with the 5th Earl but James VI allowed the titles and estates to pass through the female line to a grandson Alexander Seton, who assumed the Montgomerie surname. In 1839 Archibald, 13th Earl, held here the famous Eglinton tournament as a re-enactment of those of medieval times.

FAIRLIE NS 213549

Beside a glen overlooking Fairlie Roads is a roofless but well preserved tower of c1500. It was built by the Fairlies, supposedly descended from the Rosses of Tarbet. In 1650 the last Fairlie sold it to John Boyle of Kelburn. The tower measures 13.8m by 8.7m over walls 1.6m thick at ground level. Each of the four storeys was subdivided and the staircase opening off the entrance lobby (the doorway itself is blocked) is placed in a side wall to make access to the western chambers easier. One of the vaulted cellars has a service stair and both have gunports. Above is a hall with a narrow kitchen at the east end. Above are pairs of private chambers with fireplaces, latrines, and pleasant seats fitted with seats. A chequer arrangement of corbels supports the parapet which has roundels at all four corners.

GIFFEN NS 377507

Giffen was a barony given to Sir Hew de Eglinton in 1370. The shapeless fallen fragments above a rock face and within a garden of a modern house are remains of a tower probably built soon after the barony was given by Sir John Montgomery of Ardrossan to his second son Sir William c1450. The Montgomeries abandoned the tower in 1722 and most of it collapsed in 1838 after a century of neglect.

Glengarnock Castle

GLENGARNOCK NS 311574

The barony of Glengarnock was held by the Cunninghames from the 13th century until the early 17th. After being abandoned in the early 18th century the castle was plundered for its materials. Set on the end of a promontory grandly situated by the ravine of the Garnock Burn is a tower house of c1380 which is 13m long by 9.7m wide with walls 1.9m thick. The landward facing wall on the east was reduced to its base when it fell in a storm in 1839 but the other walls stand to the height of the moulded string course of the parapet. The vault of the unlighted cellar probably originally only entered by a hatch and trap-door has fallen, but part remains of the pointed vault of the lofty hall above. This room had a high window in each gable and a lower window in each sidewall near the north end. A screened passage probably connected the stair leading up in the SW corner to a doorway in the east wall.

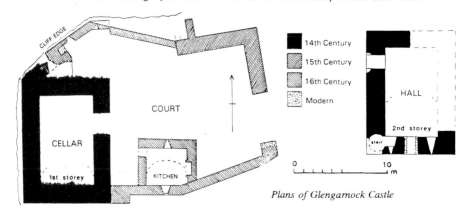

Plans of Glengarnock Castle

In the 15th century a second block of similar size was built a short distance to the east. The parts of the north and east walls that remain show that it had round bartizans with machicolation slots on the east corners. It is likely that the block contained a common hall above an entrance passage with offices or cellars on either side. The building was destroyed later except for its outer walls retained as part of the enclosing wall of the courtyard. This court must have been nearly filled with minor offices and rooms although only a 16th century vaulted kitchen now survives.

GREENAN NS 312193

Dramatically placed on the end of a ridge with a sheer drop to a beach 3.5km SW of Ayr is a ruined tower which once bore the date 1603 and the initials of John Kennedy of Baltersan. The Davidsons are said to have had an earlier fortalice on the site. A spiral stair in the NE corner connects the four storeys, the topmost of which has closets with shotholes in round bartizans on the other three corners. The entrance is now blocked up. There are traces of a hall on the west side of a court to the south.

HESSILHEAD NS 379533

Amongst shrubs by a bend in a track close to a flooded quarry pit 3km ESE of Beith are a few fallen fragments of a tower built by the Montgomeries c1500 when this part of the barony of Giffen was divided off to make an estate for a younger son. Drawings exist of the substantial ruin which survived until the beginning of the present century. In 1680 Robert Montgomerie, the last of the male line of this branch, sold Hessilhead to his relative Francis Montgomerie of Giffen who doubled the length of the building by adding a three storey extension with big windows. This new part contained a scale-and-platt staircase ascending from an entrance lobby in the middle of the building.

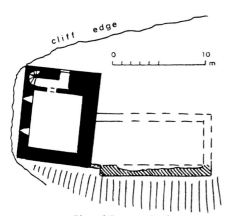

Plan of Greenan Castle

Greenan Castle

Hunterston Castle

Kilburnie Castle

HUNTERSTON NS 193515

This small estate was owned by the Hunters from an early date. In c1500 they built a four storey tower measuring 7.3m by 6.6m rising 10.2m to the top of the parapet upon a single course of plain rectangular corbels. The parapet on the east side made have been altered to be flush with the wall face below when a three storey range was added on this side in the 17th century. This range has dormer windows and a square stair turret on the south front. The tower has original entrances to the cellar and hall set one above the other in the east wall. Originally only a hatch in a vault connected these two levels. A spiral stair in the NE corner then leads from the hall to the bedrooms and battlements. Other additions have been made later and a small court created south of the tower. A range of offices to the west have been removed although there remains a large inserted doorway at ground level in tower west wall.

KELBURN NS 217567

The Boyles have owned this estate since the 12th century but the oldest building now standing is a four storey Z-planned tower house with round towers at diagonally opposite corners which bears the initials of John Boyle, laird 1583-1610, and his wife Marion Crawfurd of Kilburnie. The western tower contains a staircase and the other two corners have round bartizans, below one of which is a corbelled projection allowing sufficient wall thickness here for a mural chamber. The main block measures 15m by 8m and the towers are 4.4m in diameter. Joining the main block rather awkwardly and apparently replacing a 17th century wing is a long rectangular block with a wider middle section bearing the date 1722 and the initials of David Boyle, created Earl of Glasgow in 1703, his first wife Margaret Lindsay, and his second wife Jean, the heiress of William Mure of Rowallan. See plan p16.

Kerelaw Castle

Kelburn Castle

Plan of the Place of Kilburnie

1st Storey

STAIR

0   5
metres

■ 15th Century

▨ 17th Century

▧ Modern

KERELAW   NS 269428

A modern wall connects parts of the NE side walls of a pair of two storey ranges on either side of a court beside a small burn. One range contains has a segmental headed and roll-moulded gateway. This was a Cunninghame seat and the remains probably date from after a sacking by the Montgomeries in the 1520s in the course of a feud.

KIERS   NS 430081

The very slight traces behind an outbuilding of the farm and above the ravine of a tributary of the River Doon are said to mark the site of a small early castle of enclosure like that at Loch Doon. Clearance and excavation would now be required to prove this.

KILBIRNIE   NS 304541

The oldest part of the Place of Kilburnie by a stream west of the town is a ruined and ivy mantled tower probably built by Malcolm Crawford, a younger son of the Loudon Crawfurds, who married the Barclay heiress of Kilbirnie in the 1470s. The tower contained a cellar and sleeping loft under a vault, a hall and private room under another vault, and a fifth storey bedroom above. In the north end wall is the blocked and half buried round arched entrance. A spiral stair adjoined it in the NE corner. In the NW corner is a pit prison reached by a hatch from a passage from the stair at loft level. The hall has a large fireplace and windows in the side walls and end wall at the south end. Here a door has been broken through to give access to the staircase of an even more ruined mansion, now very choked with its own debris, built in the 1620s by John Crawfurd. It had turrets corbelled out at hall level on the southern corners to contain closets opening off each of the two upper storeys and the attics, but only the base of the western turret now remains. There was a front door in a shallow projection on the south side and a narrow back door facing north where there was presumably a court. East of the passages connecting these was a kitchen, and there were two cellars to the west with a passage behind them to connect with the main staircase.

Kilkerran Castle

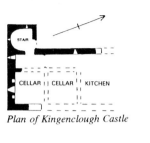

Plan of Kingenclough Castle

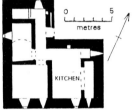

0   5
metres

KITCHEN

Plan of Kirkhill Castle

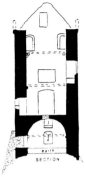

SECTION

*Plans and Section
of Kilkerran Castle*

KILHENZIE   NS 308082

In the 19th century a three storey tower with conical roofed bartizans built by John Baird, a participant in the Kennedy feuds at the close of the 16th century, was restored from ruin and incorporated into a new mansion. See photo p17.

KILKERRAN   NS 293005

Only the 6.8m wide north end now remains of a tower built by the Fergussons c1500 on bluff above the wooded ravine of a burn 2.5km SE of Dailly. After the rest fell the surviving part, which is 13m high to the wall-walk, was buttressed on the SW side. A fallen fragment of the south corner shows that it contained the spiral staircase. Below the vault supporting the hall floor the tower had a cellar and a low sleeping loft, and there were two storeys of bedrooms, plus an attic room within the battlements.

KILLOCHAN   NS 227004

The inscription over the entrance tells us that this lofty L-plan tower house with a round tower on the outermost angle was built in 1586 by John Cathcart of Carlton, his family having been in possession of the estate on the north side of the Water of Girvan since c1314. The castle passed to a junior branch of the family in 1916 and was sold to the Somervells of Sorn in 1954. The main block measures 15.8m by 8.6m and contains a kitchen and two cellars in the basement, a hall above reached by a scale-and-platt stair from the entrance in the wing, and three upper storeys of bedrooms connected by staircases in a round turret corbelled out beside the round tower and in a square turret in the re-entrant angle rising one stage above the rest of the building. There is a machicolation high above the entrance. On several of the corners are round bartizans and there were dormer windows until the roof was raised in the 17th century. The hall and wine cellar are connected by a service stair.

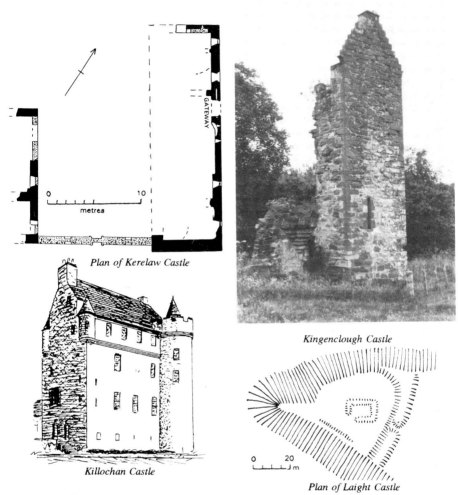

Plan of Kerelaw Castle

Kingenclough Castle

Killochan Castle

Plan of Laight Castle

KILMAURS NS 412411

This is a much altered L-plan 17th century building on the site of an older castle. A lean-to porch now lies in the re-entrant angle. This was a Cunninghame seat and from it they took their secondary title of Viscount Kilmuir.

KINGENCLOUGH NS 503256

The Campbells of Loudon built a modest L-plan house here c1620 supposedly in replacement of an earlier house in the ruin of which John Knox is said to have preached. The new house itself became a ruin after a new mansion was built on higher ground to the north in the 18th century. The wing containing the main stair from the entrance to the hall and two small upper rooms linked by a narrow stair over the re-entrant angle stands to the top of the crow-stepped gable, but only the lower parts of the adjoining walls of the main block survive. It had the usual arrangement of a passage from the stair leading past two cellars to a kitchen at the far end.

Kirkhill Castle

Law Castle

KIRKHILL   NX 146859

Kirkhill lies in the village of Colmonell and was a Kennedy seat until sold in 1843 to Lieutenant-Colonel Barton. He built the present mansion beside the L-plan tower house of three storeys with an attic in the upper part of the former roof. Over one of three large hall windows retaining their iron grilles is the date 1589 and the initials of Thomas and Janet Kennedy. From them was descended the Sir Thomas Kennedy who was Provost of Edinburgh in 1680-4. He purchased the estates of his relatives at Dunure, Dalquharran, and Girvan Mains from the proceeds of a fortune made from transhipping arms. The basement contains a kitchen and two cellars, the smallest of which is tucked under a scale-and platt staircase from the entrance to the hall. Access above was by a stair corbelled out over the re-entrant angle. Third storey closets furnished with shotholes are provided in bartizans on the southern corners.

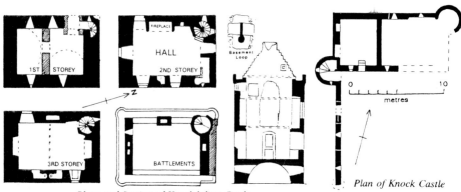

Plans and Section of Knockdolian Castle

Plan of Knock Castle

KNOCK   NS 194631

Near Robert Steel's mansion of 1850 above the coast road north of Largs are the remains of a thinly walled Z-plan castle of c1600 and one side of an adjoining block now dressed up with a turret and parapet as a garden ornament but bearing a stone with the year 1604 and the initials of one of the Frasers and his wife (probably Janet Boyle). The Frasers acquired Knock by marriage c1380 and held it until it passed to Sir Robert Montgomerie of Skelmorlie in 1674. The main block measured 13m by 6.3m and did not have a passage linking the kitchen and cellars with the staircase in the western of the two round corner turrets, as is usual. The stair still serves four storeys and an attic in the derelict western part. The remainder is much more ruined.

KNOCKDOLIAN   NX 123854

In the grounds of a modern mansion above the west bank of the River Stinchar is a ruined tower built c1500 by the Grahams. It measures 10.7m by 7.6m and rises 11.5m to the top of the parapet which has tiny roundels and surrounds an attic with stepped gables. Fergus M'Cubbin and Margaret Kennedy are known to have carried out work on the tower in the 17th century so it was presumably they who thickened the north gable at the expense of the wall-walk to help support the roof of an extension now removed. The original doorway in the north wall at hall level then gave onto the extension and it was necessary to provide a new ground floor entrance at the foot of the staircase in the NW corner. At the same time the basement, which has loops with bottom roundels, was divided by a cross wall and to give sufficient head clearance for the new doorway the northern part of the vault was rebuilt to an east-west axis. The hall has a large fireplace in the west wall, a latrine in the NE corner, and four large windows. Above is the laird's suite of two rooms each with a latrine, fireplace, and a single large window. The storey above contained two more bedrooms.

LAIGHT   NS 450089

A ditch 2m deep and 10m wide isolates a triangular platform 55m long by 38m wide high above the Dunaskin Burn. in the platform are footings of a tower about 16m long by 11m wide over walls 3m thick built by the Crawfurds probably c1370-1400.

LAINSHAW   NS 410453

A 15th century tower of the Stewarts passed to the Montgomeries in 1570. It was sold to the Cunninghames in 1779 and incorporated in a large new mansion.

LAW   NS 211484

This recently restored tower on the slope of Law Hill east of West Kilbride was built by the Boyds supposedly in 1468 for James III's sister Mary on her marriage to Thomas Boyd, although it can hardly have been completed before the Princess and her husband were forced into exile the following year. The Boyds retained possession of Law until Major Bontin obtained it from William, 3rd Earl of Kilmarnock on 1670. The tower measures 12.5m by 9.2m and rises 13.2m to a wall-walk with a parapet and roundels supported on four continuous corbelled courses. The entrance lies in the middle of the south side and has the spiral stair to one side of it instead of in a corner, an arrangement allowing easier access to all the rooms, for each of the four storeys was subdivided. The cellars have splayed gunloops. A service stair leads up to the hall which has big fireplace at the west end and a narrow kitchen with a huge fireplace in the east end wall. One hall window was later blocked to provide a niche for a date stone over the entrance. The third storey formed a suite of two rooms for the laird and the fourth storey contains two bedrooms, all these having latrines in the north wall.

LITTLE CUMBRAE NS 153514

At the north end of Castle Island east of Little Cumbrae is a ruined tower 12.5m long by 9m wide rising 13.5m to the wall-walk. The only original entrance was beside a narrow kitchen at the level of the lofty vaulted hall. A stair leads down to two vaulted cellars, and up to two bedrooms and an attic within a parapet on a chequer arrangement of corbels. The present ground floor entrance is later. The Hunters were for long guardians of Little Cumbrae but they were too weak to suppress the pirates ravaging the Firth of Clyde during the minority of James V. As a result New Montgomerie, Earl of Eglinton was made keeper of the island in 1515 and the castle was presumably built by him soon afterwards. The Montgomeries continued to use the castle until its location made it inconvenience as a residence, and here Baillie, Principal of Glasgow sought refuge with them at the time of Cromwell's invasion of Scotland.

LOCH DOON   NX 483950

This remotely sited ruin stood on an island in Loch Doon until the 1880s when it was rebuilt on the shore above a planned rise in the water level to help supply the town of Ayr. It seems to have formed a frontier post and hunting lodge at the meeting of the bounds of Carrick, Kyle Regis and Galloway and is assumed to have been built in the 1280s by Robert, Earl of Carrick, although it just possible that Alexander III was the builder. A curtain wall faced with fine ashlar and 2.2m thick above a battered plinth encloses a polygonal court with a maximum diameter of 23m. On the north is a pointed arched gateway 2.7m wide with a portcullis groove and on the east is a narrow postern. An unsuccessful attempt was once made to rescue the portcullis after it was discovered at the bottom of the lake. On the south side of the court are thin footings of a hall 15m long by 4.8m wide which was perhaps timber framed, and there are similar footings of a service range between the gateway and postern. On the west is the lower part of a 16th century tower house 7m wide abutted rather awkwardly against the outer wall in which is a re-set fireplace. Parts of this tower stood four storeys high before the rebuilding. A fragment remains of the entrance and stair.

After Robert Bruce's defeat at Methven in 1306 his brother-in-law Sir Christopher Seton took refuge at the castle with its hereditary captain Sir Gilbert de Carrick. After a short siege the castle was surrendered to the English who hanged Seton at Dumfries as a traitor. The castle was held for David II against Edward Balliol in 1333 and was later held by de Carrick's descendants the Kennedys. In 1510 William Crawfurd of Lochmores temporarily took possession of the castle. It is supposed to have been gutted by fire in the 1530s but was restored and occupied until the 17th century.

Loch Doon Castle

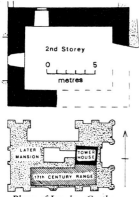

Plans of Loudon Castle

Mauchline Castle

LOUDON NS 506378

In 1981 a tree-clad motte with traces of stonework was identified to the east of the large overgrown ruined mansion NE of Galston. The mansion is built around a Crawfurd tower probably built soon after a Kennedy raid in the 1480s. It measured 13m by 10.5m over walls 1.8m thick and had vaults over the first and third of four storeys. The SE corner which contained the stair is now missing above the lower vault and only a high dramatic fragment remains of three extra upper storeys added c1820. The castle later passed to the Campbells, Hew Campbell being created Lord Loudon in 1601. His granddaughter married John Campbell who was Chancellor of Scotland under Charles I and was created Earl of Loudon in 1633. Only the very altered basement survives of the 36m long wing he added to the south and SW of the tower. The Countess of Loudon surrendered the castle to Cromwell's forces in 1650 after a short siege. The Earl took part in the Royalist rising led by Glencairn in 1653. Flora, heiress of the 5th Earl, married Francis, Earl of Moira, created Marquis of Hastings in 1817. Although they mostly lived abroad they engulfed the old parts in a new castellated mansion. When Henry, 4th Marquis died in 1868 the senior title became extinct but the earldom passed via a female to a line who lived here until the 1940s.

MARTNAHAM NS 395173

On a densely wooden promontory which was probably once an island in Martnaham Loch are the lower parts of building of uncertain date 21.4m long by 7.3m wide over walls 0.8m thick. It is divided into three, the smallest room on the SW having what may be a fireplace in the crosswall. A stone causeway leads to the building.

MAUCHLINE NS 496273

The late 15th century tower by a stream in the town formed the residence of the prior of a cell of Melrose Abbey. The tower was later held by the Campbells of Loudon and in the late 18th century was owned by Gavin Hamilton who was an early patron of Burns. The poet lived for a time in the tower and was married in a room in a southerly extension of later date still occupied as a private residence. The tower retains its roof although only the corbels remain of the parapet around the topmost of the three rooms. The tower measures 10.5m by 9m over walls 1.5m thick and has vaults over the two main rooms, the top vault being in two quadripartite bays. Both rooms are well lighted apartments with latrines in a projection in the north end wall. The lower room windows have rare round heads to the lights, arranged both singly and in pairs.

Monk Castle

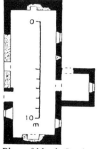

Plan of Monk Castle

Plan of Newmilns Tower

Maybole
Castle

MAYBOLE   NS 301100

This noble L-plan tower was the town house of the Earls of Cassillis. It was probably erected in the 1620s by John, 6th Earl, who was more peaceable and virtuous than his feuding ancestors and became President of the Court. In the 1650s he was sent to confer with the exiled Charles II and at The Restoration he was appointed Extraordinary Lord of Session. In the 19th century the tower was restored and low wings added for occupation by factors serving the Earls. The tower measures 11.8m by 8m and has a stair wing 4.4. wide projecting 3.6m. The fourth storey in the roof has dormer windows with finely decorated pediments and closets in round bartizans on the east corners while over the stair at this level is corbelled-out caphouse forming a study with a three sided oriel window in the end gable. The much altered staircase tower embellished with a clock and now called The tollbooth is a relic of a town house of the laird of Blairquhan. Baird of Kilhenzie, the Abbot of Crossraguel and the Kennedy lairds of Knockdone, Culzean, and Ballimore all once had town houses at Maybole.

MONK   NS 292474

An estate once belonging to Kilwinning Abbey was acquired in 1552 by the Duke of Chatelherault. He gave it to his younger son Claude Hamilton, Commendator of Paisley Abbey. It was probably Claude's son, who became Earl of Abercorn and Baron Monkcastle, who built the existing T-planned building c1620 probably as a dower house or occasional retreat since he had several other seats. The much rebuilt and gutted house is 15m long by 6.3m wide and has a square stair turret near the middle of the south side. Above the entrance are crude carvings of a human head and lizards with human heads. Flanking the entrance is a loop with a bottom roundel, possibly re-set from an older building of c1500. The inner embrasure cannot now be traced.

MONKREDDING   NS 324455

In 1532 Thomas Nevan obtained lands here from nearby Kilwinning Abbey. A descendant built a small tower which is dated 1602 and has a southern extension dated 1638. These now form the west wing of a U-shaped mansion built by the Cunninghames of Clonbeith to whom the estate passed in 1698.

MONTFODE NS 226441

In a field 2km north of Ardrossan Ferry Terminal is a ruined stair turret 3.6m diameter, the last relic of a small tower house of c1600 probably built by a cadet of the Montgomeries of Ardrossan. The turret contains the entrance doorway and a gunport.

NEWARK NS 324173

Perched on a small 2m high crag is a still inhabited tower house of c1500 measuring 9.7m by 8.2m. It has a vaulted cellar, three upper storeys, and an attic within a somewhat altered parapet with corner roundels. Newark was a jointure house given to the spouses of the Kennedy lairds of Bargany. One of its occupants was "Black Bessie" Kennedy of Brunston over whose lands a private war was fought between Lord Bargany and The Earl of Cassillis. After the Earl's ally Sir Thomas Kennedy of Culzean was murdered in 1602 the laird of Auchindrayne, said to be an accomplice of the killers, took refuge here with the then proprietor Duncan Crawfurd and attacks by the Earl's forces were repulsed. A doorway at the head of a former outside stair once bore an inscription relating the marriage of James Crawfurd and Anna Kennedy in 1687 and their purchase of the castle in that year. It may have been them who built the western extension. The castle was extended to the north in the 19th century.

NEWMILNS NS 536374

In the back yard of a public house off Castle Street in the town is a decayed but still roofed tower of three storeys and an attic built c1550 by the Campbells of Loudon. It was occupied by a Captain Inglis in the late 17th century when Covenanters were incarcerated within it. In latter years it has served merely as a store and has lost the parapet and roundels although the continuous corbelled coursing for them remains. The tower measures 8.4m by 7m and has a staircase in the SE corner next to the round headed entrance over which is a blank niche for a date stone. String courses on the side walls mark the position of the floors of the upper rooms.

Newark Castle

Newmilns Tower

PENKILL   NS 232985

The Boyds obtained Penkill in the early 16th century and in c1600 built a four storey tower by a tributary of the Penwhapple Burn. The tower measures 8m by 6.5m and has on the SE and NE corners which face the approach a round bartizan and staircase tower respectively. A range 6m wide extending to the NE was added in 1628 by Thomas Boyd after his marriage with Marion Mure of Rowallan. In the mid 19th century G.E.Street tidied up the ruin for Spencer Boyd. What remained of the later block then becoming part of the main building, the stair tower of which gained a projecting upper storey with a still further projecting parapet above, while a lower wing was built on the footings of the eastern part of the later wing. The rebuilt castle became a haunt of Pre-Raphaelite artists such as Dante Gabriel Rossetti and his sister Christina. It is a private residence but is open to the public by appointment in summer.

PINMORE   NX 206904

A modern house on a shelf above bend of the River Stinchar stands on the site of an old house of the Hamiltons destroyed by fire in 1874 and replaced soon afterwards.

PINWHERRY   NX 198867

A tree-clad hillock by the Duisk River near its junction with the River Stinchar bears an ivy-mantled ruin of an L-planned tower house held by Johnnie Kennedy in the 1590s and probably built by him. After Thomas Kennedy died in 1644 "Banquharrie" or "Pinquharrie" eventually passed to John, Earl of Carrick. It then passed through various hands and was superseded by a nearby 19th century house. The main block measures 9.7m by 7.4m and has four storeys including an attic high in the roof. A bartizan contains a SW corner closet off one of the third storey bedrooms. From the hall a service stair in the SW corner and a wider stair in the wing lead down and a narrow stair corbelled out over the re-entrant angle leads up.

Penkill Castle

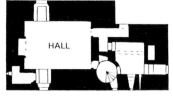

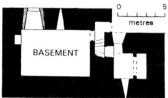

Rowallan Castle

Plans of Portincross Castle

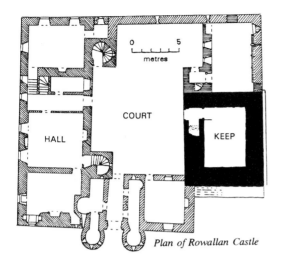

Plan of Rowallan Castle

Portincross Castle

■ 13th Century

▨ Late 16th Century

▨ 16th Century

≡ 17th Century

▦ Modern

PORTINCROSS NS 176488

This castle on the rocky shore near West Kilbride was the seat of the barony of Arnele conferred by Robert I on Sir Robert Boyd of Kilmarnock. Robert II and III were frequent visitors when in transit between their favourite residences of Dundonald on the mainland and Rothesay on the Isle of Bute. The castle may have been built for their use and this would explain some unusual arrangements within it. It remained a Boyd property until 1737 but from the 1600s it was inhabited only by fishermen until the roof was blown off in 1739. The shell, however, remains fairly complete. It consists of a block 12m by 9.5m with walls 2.3m thick containing basement and a lofty hall both with barrel vaults, and an attic serving as a barrack room in the gables. Continuing the length of the block for a further 5.7m is a higher wing 7m wide containing two kitchens and two upper storeys forming a suite of private rooms linked by a wide spiral staircase to each other, the hall, the battlements, and by a straight stair to the entrance at ground level. A second upper entrance leads via a passage direct to the hall which has a fireplace in the end wall and windows with seats in each side wall, off one of which is a latrine. The hall and private rooms could be served by either of the kitchens. Although unheated, and dark until a window was inserted later, the basement may have been intended as a living room for those of lesser rank.

ROBERTLAND NS 441470

An altered 16th century tower stands above the Swinzie Burn 2km NE of Stewarton.

ROWALLAN A.M. NS 435424

The mound on which the castle stands is probably a 12th century motte originally surrounded by marsh or open water, there being streams to the NE and SE. Alexander III rewarded Gilcrist Muir for is part in the victory against the Norsemen at Largs in 1263 with the hand of Comyn heiress of Rowallan. On the north side of the mound is the very ruined lower part of a tower house 10m long by 8.7m wide which may have been built soon afterwards. The basement is full of earth and rubble and the only surviving features are the entrance and straight mural stair in the south wall. The most famous of the Muirs was Elizabeth, first wife of Robert Stewart. She died before he became King but her eldest son succeeded to the throne as Robert III.

The main apartments at Rowallan lie in still roofed south range 22m long and 8m wide separated from the old tower by a 10m wide courtyard. These were built by Mungo Muir who became laird when his father was killed at Flodden in 1513 and was himself killed in 1547 at the Battle of Pinkie. The range has a central hall with living rooms at either end at courtyard level, bedrooms above reached by square staircase turrets facing the court, and a kitchen and cellars below courtyard level. The windows all open away from the court. The east range with a gateway passage flanked by round turrets with cable mouldings and approached by a flight of 21 steps bears the date 1562 (or 7) and abbreviated forms of the names of John Muir and Marion Cunninghame. The west wall of the court with two gunports and a wall-walk is of the same period as when the grounds were laid out. Sir William Muir, laird 1639-57, added a new kitchen in the NW corner of the court. It is entered through a porch bearing arms and the initials of him and his wife Dame Jane Hamilton. A monogram of their son Sir William, a noted Covenanter, and his wife Dame Elizabeth Hamilton with the date 1661 appear on the walling containing a gateway which is all that remains of an outer court. In the 19th century Rowallan was held by the Earl of Loudon.

SKELMORLIE NS 195658

The castle lies high above the Skelmorlie Water near where it joins the sea. In c1460 the estate was divided between the Montgomeries and Cunninghames, the castle being built c1502 by a younger brother of Hew, Earl of Eglinton. Robert Montgomerie, a descendant of the builder, was made a baronet in 1628. The title became extinct in 1735 and Skelmorlie reverted to the Earls of Eglinton. In the mid 19th century it was leased to a the Glasgow merchant John Graham who restored the castle and added a large wing on the south side where there was originally a courtyard, one round tower with gunports from it still surviving at the SW corner. The tower house measures 14.6m by 8.7m and has four storeys including an attic high in the roof. Bartizans were provided in a remodelling c1600 when the original wall-walk and parapet was removed. As at Fairlie and Law the stair is contained in a side wall rather than in a corner to facilitate direct access to various rooms on each level. Here, however there is a second spiral stair from the hall to the western upper rooms in the NW corner and there is no service stair to the wine cellar. There is a tiny kitchen at the east end of the hall with third storey mural rooms on either side of its fireplace flue.

Skelmorlie Castle

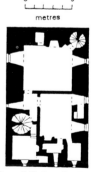

0   5
metres

Plan of Skelmorlie Castle

SORN NS 548269

Andrew, third son of Sir David Hamilton of Cadzow, acquired Sorn from the Keiths in 1406. It passed from the Hamiltons by marriage to the Seton Earl of Winton in 1585 and in the early 17th century was sold to the Earl of Loudon. A small tower built on the north bank of the River Ayr c1500 was extended to the NE to make a block 19.5m long a few years later, the whole being united with a continuous parapet with roundels on ornamental corbelling. The extension contains a hall 8.7m by 5.1m over a pair of cellars and a small kitchen, and has a third storey of bedrooms plus attics above. There are 19th century additions towards the approach on the NW side.

STAIR NS 442239

Stair was held by the Montgomeries originally and in 1450 passed to William Dalrymple on his marriage to the heiress Agnes Kennedy. The present house south of a loop of the River Ayr and north of the village is largely the work of James Dalrymple, a soldier, philosopher, and legal expert, who was created Viscount Stair by Charles II and lived until 1695. The core of the building is a low three storey tower house with square wing at the SE corner and a four stage round tower at the NW corner likely to have been erected about the time of his birth in 1619. The extensions comprise a three storey NW range with a round tower at the far corner and a two storey range with another conical roofed tower to the SW.

STANE NS 338399

A four storey tower built c1520 by a cadet of the Montgomeries of Eglinton survives roofless but complete apart from the gables of the attic within the parapet and roundels on ornamental corbelling. In c1750 Alexander, 10th Earl of Eglinton adopted it as an ornament in the grounds of Eglinton Castle to the NW. He introduced the large pointed blank recesses and centrally placed windows. The only original features surviving apart from the spiral stair in the NE corner are the doorway and one window on the south side at hall level and a pair of small windows in each side wall at the top.

Stane Castle

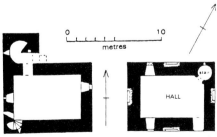

Plan of Pinwherry Castle   *Plan of Stane Castle*

SUNDRUM   NS 410213

Most of this plain building above the tree-clad south bank of the Water of Coyle 3.5km SW of Stair was built in 1793 by the 1st Lord Hamilton of Sundrum. It incorporates a tower house with walls 3m thick which may date back to the time of Sir Duncan Wallace, who was granted a charter of the estate in 1373. It later passed to the Cathcarts, went to the Hamiltons in 1750, and now serves as a hotel.

TERRINGZEAN   NS 556205

On level ground above the south side of the Lugar Water 1.5km west of Cumnock are remains of an unusual castle about which little is known other than that the Crawfurds held it in later years. The site is protected by a dry ditch to the SW. The best preserved part is an ashlar faced octagonal tower 9m across above a stepped and chamfered plinth. The tower probably dates from c1380 and has a spiral stair beside an entrance into a rectangular basement formerly covered by a vault with three chamfered ribs and having what may have been a well recess. The larger room above has a south window and a latrine on the east. There are no signs of any contemporary courtyard walls joining the north side of the tower or of a gateway passage beside it as might be expected and the plinth continues uninterrupted on that side but on the west a wall 2.3m thick and now 1m high connects it to the only surviving corner of what appears to have been an earlier hall-house 23m long by 10m wide with walls 2.1m thick. In the late 16th or early 17th century a thinly walled block 18.6m long by 6.8m wide was built over the site of the hall block west wall, although a long featureless section of the east wall was rather oddly left standing just 3m in front of it. Of about the same period are traces of a range to the north of the octagonal tower.

Terringzean Castle

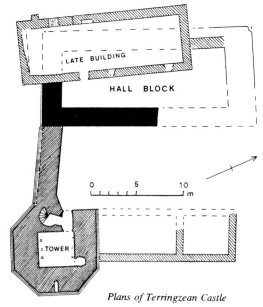

LATE BUILDING

HALL   BLOCK

0   5   10
m

TOWER

Plans of Terringzean Castle

Thomaston Castle

THOMASTON   NS 240096

Beside kennels by the coast road 1km SE of Culzean Castle is a castle probably built by Thomas Corry who was granted the estate in 1507. In the mid 17th century it passed to the MacIlvanes of Grimmet who held the castle for about a century. It remained inhabited until c1800 and the ruined shell is fairly complete except for the gables of the attics and parapets with roundels on continuous corbelled courses. It consists of a main block 17.8m long by 7.9m wide with a wing 5m wide projecting 5.5m from the south side to contain at ground level a vaulted passage into a now destroyed courtyard and small private rooms above. Adjoining the wing was a range to the south now only represented by a scar of its roof and a doorway to the entrance passage. In the re-entrant angle between the wing and main block is a square stair turret with the entrance at its foot. From it led a passage connecting three cellars and a larger room, perhaps a kitchen, although it lacks a fireplace. The wine cellar at the west end has a pair of double splayed gunports and a service stair up to the private room divided off at this end of the hall. The third storey contained several bedrooms.

TRABBOCH   NS 448222

By the Trabboch Burn 2.3km Se of stair are the defaced lower parts of two 2.5m thick walls of a 15th century tower 10.5m wide and probably about 15m long.

TREESBANK   NS 420346

A 16th century tower house is incorporated in the house built by the first of the Campbells of Treesbank in 1672. The house was enlarged in 1838.

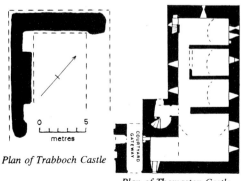

Plan of Trabboch Castle

Plan of Thomaston Castle

TURNBERRY   NS 196073

Surrounding the lighthouse on a low rocky headland are the lower parts of the walls of a substantial 13th century castle which was the chief seat of the early Earls of Carrick. The building may have been begun either by Duncan, made Earl by William the Lion, or his son Neil, who died in 1256. Neil's daughter Marjorie married firstly Adam de Kilconquhar, who was 3rd Earl until his death in 1270, and secondly the 6th Robert Bruce of Annandale, who thus became 4th Earl of Carrick, although the headship of Marjorie's family went to someone else who took the surname de Carrick and is thought to have been the ancestor of the Kennedys. Robert may have built much of what is now visible but considerable clearance would be required to show what was built when. The castle was presumably destroyed by Robert, 5th Earl of Carrick during his struggles with the English after seizing the Scottish throne, and there does not appear to be any historical or structural evidence of subsequent use of the site.

The site comprises two parts naturally divided by a gully descending almost to sea-level. To the north was the small inner ward on the highest part of the rock while for 55m to the south extended the outer ward of which little remains apart from the base of the thick east wall with a ditch in front of it. On the north side of where the modern road to the lighthouse enters the site is the jamb of the outer gate with a portcullis groove. A timber ramp led up to the inner ward gate which was flanked on the west by a tower 6m square and on the other side by an eastward facing D-shaped tower 12m in diameter which presumably formed a keep. On the north side of the tiny court is a high fragment of a former block of apartments. The court was small because part of the space enclosed within the walls was actually a chasm descending to sea level and isolating the keep. North of the keep two walls crossed the chasm on high arches to form a sort of boat house into which sea going vessels could sail and unload. This arrangement recalls the docking facilities of Edward I's series of castles in North Wales begun in 1277, and is likely to be of the time of the 4th and 5th Earls of Carrick.

LIST OF EARTHWORKS

ALLOWAY NS 338180 Small mound in trees by bend of Doon 0.7km E old church.

ALMONT NX 187873 Mound 2m high bearing monument to John Snell (1629-79).

CHAPELTOUN NS 393442 Small mound by Chapeltoun House 3km SW of Stewarton.

DALMELLINGTON NS 482058 Fine mound above Muck Water at frontier of Carrick and Galloway. It rises 8m above the ditch to a summit 19m across.

DINVIN NS 450089 Huge mound 7m high above inner of two ditches with bank 4m high between them and a counterscarp beyond. Summit 30m by 19m.

DORNAL NS 632194 Long narrow mound 5m high by bend of Glenmuir Water.

HELENTON NS 394311 Tree-clad mound 3m high above adjacent road with irregular summit 19m by 17m by Pow Burn 1km Se of Symington.

IRVINE NS 342356 This mound may be the castle mentioned in a document of 1184.

MONTFODE NS 226437 Treeclad motte 26m by 21m on top. 2m high towards ridge but 6m high to south. By a stream 0.4km south of Montfode Castle.

MOTE KNOWE NS 297002 Natural knoll above Dobbingstone Burn 3km SE of Dailly. Summit 30m long by 6m wide mostly 6m high except on east.

NETHERSHIELD NS 586263 Site only by River Ayr and a burn SE of the farm.

OCHILTREE NS 504216 D-shaped platform 18m by 16m above drop to Lugar Water 0.5km NW of Ochiltree. Ditch 2m deep on the other sides.

SHANTER KNOWE NS 218074 Mound 3 to 4m high with summit 9m across on high ground 2.2km east of Turnberry Castle.

STEWARTON NS 411447 Mound 4m high to summit 13m across 1.3km SW of town.

TARBOLTON NS 433274 Motte 2.5m high with summit 12m in diameter NE corner of bailey platform 55m by 40m within band of B744 north of village.

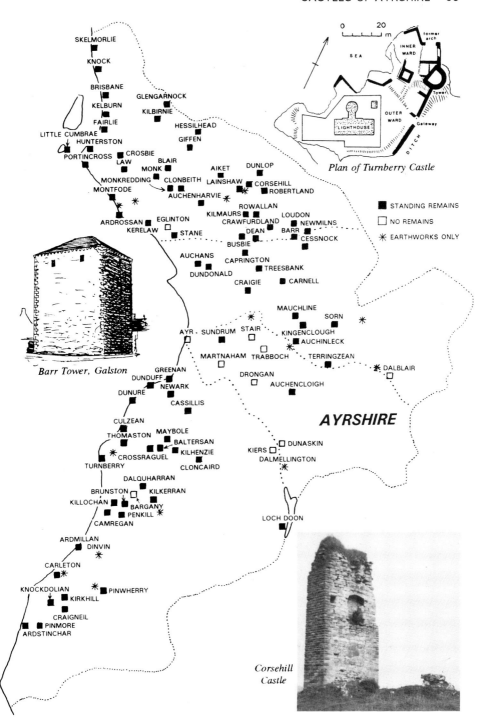

0   20
m

SEA

INNER WARD

former arch

LIGHTHOUSE

OUTER WARD

Tower

Gateway

DITCH

Plan of Turnberry Castle

SKELMORLIE
KNOCK
BRISBANE
KELBURN
GLENGARNOCK
KILBIRNIE
FAIRLIE
HESSILHEAD
LITTLE CUMBRAE
HUNTERSTON
GIFFEN
PORTINCROSS
CROSBIE
LAW   BLAIR
MONK
AIKET   DUNLOP
MONKREDDING
CLONBEITH   LAINSHAW
CORSEHILL
MONTFODE
AUCHENHARVIE   ✳   ROBERTLAND
ARDROSSAN   EGLINTON
ROWALLAN
KILMAURS   LOUDON
KERELAW
CRAWFURDLAND   NEWMILNS
STANE   DEAN   BARR
BUSBIE   CESSNOCK
AUCHANS
CAPRINGTON
DUNDONALD   TREESBANK
CRAIGIE   CARNELL

MAUCHLINE
SORN
AYR   SUNDRUM   STAIR
KINGENCLOUGH
AUCHINLECK
MARTNAHAM   TRABBOCH   TERRINGZEAN
DALBLAIR
GREENAN
DUNDUFF   DRONGAN
DUNURE   NEWARK
AUCHENCLOIGH
CASSILLIS

AYRSHIRE

CULZEAN
THOMASTON   MAYBOLE
BALTERSAN
CROSSRAGUEL   KILHENZIE
DUNASKIN
KIERS
TURNBERRY   CLONCAIRD
DALMELLINGTON
DALQUHARRAN
BRUNSTON   KILKERRAN
KILLOCHAN
BARGANY
PENKILL
CAMREGAN   LOCH DOON
ARDMILLAN
DINVIN
CARLETON
KNOCKDOLIAN   PINWHERRY
KIRKHILL
CRAIGNEIL
PINMORE
ARDSTINCHAR

■ STANDING REMAINS
□ NO REMAINS
✳ EARTHWORKS ONLY

Barr Tower, Galston

Corsehill Castle

GAZETTEER OF CASTLES IN DUMFRIESSHIRE

AMISFIELD NX 992838

Panels on the four storey tower with an unusually picturesque summit outline bear the arms and initials of John Charteris whose family held Amisfield from an early date, and those of his wife Agnes Maxwell, plus the year 1600. The massive and plain lower parts of the tower with a straight stair connecting the entrance to the foot of a spiral stair is early 16th century so the grandiose upper parts represent a later remodelling. The spiral stair is contained in a round turret starting above ground. It is surmounted by a two storey caphouse adjoining which is a still higher and smaller caphouse set upon one of the main gables. The other three corners have round bartizans squared off towards the end walls and containing shotholes, and there is an attic lighted by dormer windows. In 1636 Sir John Charteris and his heir (another John) resigned the barony of Amisfield, which passed to John Dalziel of Newton.

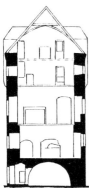

ANNAN NY 192668

The western half of the motte with a 17m diameter summit and the 77m long bailey of the original main seat of the de Brus family were eroded away by the River Annan within a couple of generations or so of being built. The church tower was regarded as a secondary strongpoint in the town and was stocked with arms by Edward I in 1299. It was destroyed during an English attack of 1547, and in the 1560s Lord Herries built a large new tower house elsewhere in the town. It must have had a barmkin of some size as it was reported to be capable of holding 100 men and 40 or 50 horses but it has been entirely destroyed.

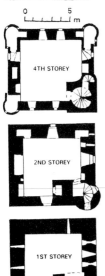

0   5
└┴┴┴┴┴┘ m

4TH STOREY

2ND STOREY

1ST STOREY

*Plans and Section
of Amisfield Tower*

Annan Motte

Auchan Castle

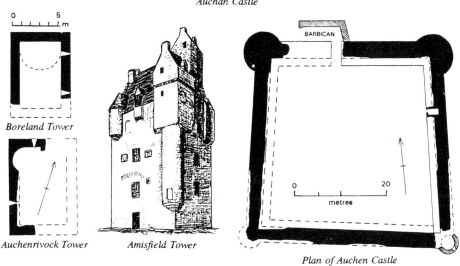

Boreland Tower

Auchenrivock Tower   *Amisfield Tower*

Plan of Auchen Castle

AUCHAN   NY 063035

Surrounding a court about 34m square are walls of the exceptional thickness of 4.5m at the base reducing to about 3m by means of an internal offset at about head height, above which level they are very ruined. There are no signs of any internal buildings which must have been of more perishable materials. The gateway in the north wall is protected by a barbican entered from the west. The northern corners have solid round towers about 9m in diameter lacking any features except a latrine shoot in the western tower which suggests they contained living rooms at levels above that to which they now stand. The southern corners have turrets about 4.5m in diameter originally probably solid although that on the SE has been rebuilt with thin and crude walling around a small circular room. The castle is generally assumed to have been built in the 1280s or 90s but the thinner walling above the offset, if not the whole of the walls, is perhaps more likely to date from the mid to late 14th century, i.e the time of Edward III's new stone walls at Lochmaben. Auchen was held successively by the Earls of Moray and Morton and then passed to the Maitlands in the 15th century. See p3.

AUCHENRIVOCK   NY 373805

Only a fragment now remains of a tower of the Irvines originally called Stakeheugh. It or a previous tower on this site was burnt in 1513 by Christopher Dacre.

BARJARG   NX 876901

Barjarg is said to have been given to Thomas Grierson by the Earl of Morton in 1587 and a stone dated 1603 with initials perhaps referring to Robert Maxwell may relate to the construction of the L-planned tower measuring 6.1m by 4m within walls 1.2m to 1.6m thick. The tower retains a yett in the entrance and has a vaulted basement. The original stair in the re-entrance angle has been replaced by a later stair in a circular turret entered from the wing. there are round bartizans containing closets opening off the attic. Adjoining the tower is a still inhabited three storey house and beyond that a modern stableblock bearing a reset panel with the year 1680 and the initials of John Grierson and Grizzel Kirkpatrick.

BARNTALLOCK   NY 353878

A fragment of a late tower house about 6m wide lies in the SW corner of the triangular motte summit which is 30m long and rises about 30m above the confluence of the River Esk and a tributary burn. A lozenge shaped bailey 66m by 33m lies to the west.

Blackwood Tower

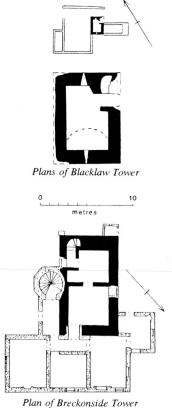

Plans of Blacklaw Tower

0 ———————————— 10
metres

Plan of Breckonside Tower

Bonshaw Tower

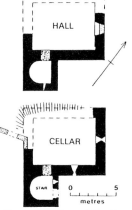

Plans of Blackwood Tower

BLACKLAW   NT 052067

The vaulted basement of a tower 9.6m by 7.3m lies on the SE side of the footings of a court 23m by 15m with a building projecting from the southern half of the NW side. The tower entrance lies away from the court beside foundations of a later wing projecting 13m from the tower.

BLACKWOOD   NY 243743

Blackwood or Blackett was an L-plan tower probably built by William Bell who was its owner in 1584. The stair wing still stands high but of the main block only the adjoining walls survive, with gunports in the basement. A length of later adjoining walling has a doorway upon which are reset stones with the dates 1663 and 1714 with the intials of John or James and George Bell and their respective wives.

BOGRIE   NX 813849

The tower was later reduced to a two storey shepherd's house and was partly dismantled in 1860. The existing building has a defaced stone with the year 1770 and the initials I.B.W. with a shield, which another over the back door has initials I.K.I.M. thought to refer to John Kirko and Jean Maxwell lived here in the 1630s. Bogrie subsequently passed by marriage to the Gordons of Lochinvar.

BONSHAW   NY 243721

The Irvines inherited Bonshaw from the Corries in the late 15th century and it became one of their chief seats. The present tower may date from immediately after the house or tower then standing high above the Kirtle Water was burnt in 1544 by the English West March Warden, Lord Wharton. The tower twice successfully resisted assaults by Lord Maxwell in 1585 and in the following year Captain Richard Maxwell was confined in it after being wounded and captured by the Johnstones. The tower measures 11m by 8m and rises 12m to a flat topped parapet carried on a corbel table. The vaulted basement has a stone bin on the east side, a prison in the SW corner, and a double splayed gunloop in each wall. Above are a hall with a fine fireplace at the south end, a bedroom with a latrine in the NW corner, and a poorly lighted attic in the roof. In the 19th century the original roof flagstones were removed to floor a farm building and slates put on in their place, whilst the parapet was heavily repaired. The building is still inhabited now.

BORELAND   NY 066958

Only the vaulted basement, now lacking the west wall, remains of a tower 9m long by 6.5m wide over walls 1m thick. There are two narrow loops in the south wall.

BRECKONSIDE   NX 841889

This derelict late 16th century tower near Moffat was a Johnstone seat. It measures 10.5m by 6.4m and has been much altered except for the two vaulted cellars. New windows have been inserted, an octagonal stair turret added in the middle of the south side and there are lower extensions at the east end.

BRECONSIDE   NT 109022

Only footings survive of a tower 8.7m by 6.3m. with traces of adjacent outbuildings. John Maxwell of "Brakensyd" was among those supporting the English in 1552.

Breckonside Tower

17th Century range, Caerlaverock

The Gatehouse,
Caerlaverock

CAERLAVEROCK NY 026656

Caerlaverock Castle has a very unusual layout. Walls about 2m thick rising directly from the waters of a moat enclose a triangular court. The south side measures 42m long internally and has a round tower 6.5m in diameter at each end. The other sides are slightly shorter and are in any case truncated because the north corner has a gatehouse with somewhat larger towers flanking a passageway which continues through a nearly rectangular inner part containing guardrooms and a hall above. The latter formed the main room of what was a complete private suite for the commander.

The present castle is thought to have been built in the 1290s by the English or a a renegade Scot as a bridgehead. The rectangular moated platform some way to the SE with traces of a rectangular stone tower 6m wide on the east is a relic of an older 13th century castle or possibly may be a site briefly in use during one of the periods in the 14th century when the present castle was in ruins. Whatever its origins and purpose Caerlaverock held a Scottish garrison in 1300 when it was beieged and captured by Edward I of England. A contemporary poem describing the siege mentions the strength of the site because of the marshes between it and the sea and clearly refers to the present castle. The castle then remained an English strongpoint until 1312 when the commander Sir Eustace Maxwell threw in his lot with Robert Bruce. He successfully resisted an English attack but subsequently demolished the castle in keeping with Bruce's policy of not leaving intact strongholds for the English to use. The result is that of this earliest period only the lower parts of the west wall and the towers at either end of it survive above the foundations. See the plan on page 9.

In the 1330s the Maxwells rebuilt the castle retaining the original layout and much of the south and east walls, the SE tower, and parts of the western curtain and towers are of that period. Herbert Maxwell submitted to Edward III of England in 1347 and in 1357 Roger Kirkpatrick captured the castle for the Scottish Crown. It was again dismantled presumably after Roger was murdered in the castle by James Lindsey. The castle may have been repaired again by the 1370s but the next evidence of it being in use does not occur until 1425 when Murdoch, Duke of Albany is said to have been confined in the SW tower which bears his name. The repairs included patching the west curtain and rebuilding the east tower of the gatehouse.There was further rebuilding in 1452-88 the period of Robert, 2nd Lord Maxwell. He added the machicolated parapets on the towers, remodelled the gatehouse into a tower house with small extensions both towards the field and the court, and built a range of other pleasant rooms for guests and other household members on the west side of the court.

James V visited the castle prior to his defeat at Solway Moss in 1542. It was surrendered to the English in 1545 as part of a negotiated agreement but later recaptured by the Scots only to be captured and wrecked by an English force led by the Earl of Sussex in 1570. Works in hand for Lord Maxwell in 1593 are likely to have included the wide mouthed gunports inserted in the gatehouse towers and the central caphouse with tiny round corner bartizans. The splendid block of residential apartments on the east side of the court bears the date 1634 about which time Robert Maxwell was created Earl of Nithsdale by Charles I. The doorways and windows have segmental and triangular tympani adorned with a variety of carved motifs such as two crows picking out the eyes of a dead man. This range took over the function originally formed by the suite in the gatehouse and contains kitchen at ground level. A spacious new hall and other apartments were created in the wide south range, now very ruined.

In September 1640 the Earl and his garrison of 200 men surrendered the castle to a force of Covenanters led by Colonel John Hume after a siege of thirteen weeks after which it was dismantled by demolishing the south wall and SE tower and unroofing the rest. By the late 18th century the ruin was already popular with visitors and the Duke of Norfolk transferred it to the Ministry of Works for preservation in 1946.

Closeburn Castle

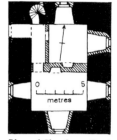

Plan of Closeburn Castle

CASTLEMILK   NY 150775

A drawing of 1547 shows the still surviving motte, which is mentioned in a document of 1174, bearing a gabled cubical tower with a round arched doorway reached by a ladder set within a low barmkin wall entered through a square gateway.

CLOSEBURN   NX 907921

The Kirkpatricks held Closeburn from at least the early 14th century, when one of then fatally stabbed Red Comyn in the Greyfriars Church at Dumfries, until they sold the estate in 1783 to Dr James Stewart Menteith. The peninsular projecting into a now drained loch originally bore a timber palisade, later replaced by a stone barmkin with round turrets. The tower dates from c1380-1420 and has walls 3m thick reduced to 2.2m further up. It measures 14.5m by 10.5m and rises 15m to the top of the existing later parapet. There are vaults over the basement, now divided into two cellars and a prison, the hall above, also later subdivided, and the fifth storey which is a servants' sleeping loft at the level of the parapet. The staircase has a later square turret on top of it and starts only at the level of the hall, where there is an entrance still retaining a yett. The basement has its own separate entrance and has no communication with the upper storeys. After a new adjoining mansion of c1600 was destroyed by fire in 1748 the tower was re-occupied for a while until a new house was built.

COMLONGON   NY 079690

In the 14th century Thomas Randolph, Earl of Moray granted an estate here to his nephew William de Moriavia. His descendants the Murrays, now Earls of Mansfield, originally lived at the vanished nearby castle of Cockpool. In the mid 15th century they built the fine tower at Comlongon now lying empty beside a much later mansion. the tower measures 15m by 13m and rises 18m to the top of the parapet around three sides, the fourth or western side having a roofed gallery probably of 17th century date. The 3.2m thick walls are honeycombed with a complex series of stairs, chambers, passages and window embrasures, especially in the upper parts. The entrance, still closed by the original yett, leads into a dark cellar with a central well. A spiral stair adjoins the entrance lobby and there is a service stair in the opposite corner. Above, tucked under the vault supporting the hall floor, was a sleeping loft. Steps down from the hall lead into a guard room intermediate between floor levels. Beyond it is a prison with a latrine and a window embrasure with seats. Beneath the guard room and reached only by a hatch in the floor is a grim dungeon without openings of any kind. the hall has a tiny narrow kitchen at the west end and a fine fireplace with the royal arms at the east end. Nearby, but on the other side of the head of the service stair is a fine aumbry with a shafted and cusped head which served as a sideboard. The two storeys above were probably subdivided as they have fireplaces in each end wall.

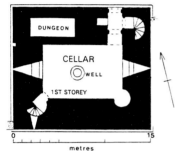

Plans of Comlongon Castle

Comlongon Castle (see also p12)

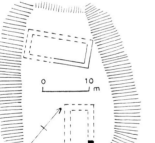

Plan of Cornal Tower

Cornal Tower

CORNAL NT 112044

The neck of a wooded promontory 35m long by 20m wide above the Cornal Burn bears footings of a building about 14m long by 6.5m wide. One fragment remains standing of a shorter building probably forming a tower in the middle of the site. Cornal belonged to the Carruthers family and later passed to the Douglases.

COSHOGLE NS 861050

Coshogle belonged to a junior branch of the Douglases of Drumlanrig. A cottage behind the steading of Coshogle Farm high above the Enterkin Burn bears shields with the date 1576 and the initials of Robert Douglas and Nichola Johnstone, and the white cottage by the farm road has a reset segmental headed doorway with moulded jambs.

COWHILL   NX 952806

An L-plan tower bearing the dates 1597 and 1611 and the initials of Robert and Barbara Maxwell was partly demolished in 1789 although the mansion intended to replace it was ultimately built elsewhere. The remaining fragment is an assembly of parts including a fragment of a round corner bartizan.

DALSWINTON   NX 945841

An early castle at Dalswinton was occupied by the English in 1309, and captured and destroyed by the Scots in 1313. It was rebuilt but destroyed again along with the castle at Dumfries in 1357 as part of the terms of David II's release from captivity in England. A later castle of c1600-20 lies hidden among shrubs in an estate. The vaulted basement kitchen, always partly below ground, is now nearly buried. At one corner is an ashlar faced round stair turret containing a moulded entrance doorway. A turret of uncertain shape at the diagonally opposite corner contained square rooms.

DRUMLANRIG   A.M.*   NX 852993

The Douglases probably built a castle here soon after 1356 when David II confirmed to them the barony of Drumlanrig granted by Robert I. Sir James Douglas, laird from 1513 to 1578, built a new hall house and palace which was destroyed in 1575. Some remains of it may be incorporated in the vaulted basement rooms of the present quadrangular mansion with ranges set around a court and rectangular corner towers. This was built in c1675-89 for William Douglas, 2nd Earl of Queensberry, elevated to a Dukedom in 1684. It has been a seat of the Dukes of Buccleugh since 1810.

DUMFRIES   NX 975754

Only mutilated earthworks remain of a royal castle which was seized by the elder Robert Bruce in 1286 after Alexander III's death. It held an English garrison of 76 men in 1298 and in 1300 was provided with a new palisade of timber from Inglewood Forest in Cumbria. The castle was briefly taken for the younger Robert Bruce after the murder of Red Comyn in 1306. It was recaptured by the English and held against Bruce until Sir Dugal MacDougall was obliged to surrender it after the English defeat at Bannockburn. The castle was finally destroyed in 1357 (see Dalswinton above).

Elshieshields Tower

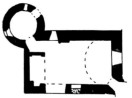

Plan of Dalswinton Castle

0   10
                     m

Plans of Fourmerkland Tower

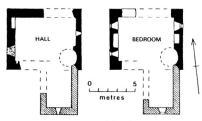

Plans of Frenchland Tower

ELLIOCK NS 796074

An H-shaped house with a round staircase tower dated MDCLVIII incorporates in the northern wing the vaulted basement with shotholes of a late 16th century tower 6.3m wide. The Dalziels held Elliock in 1388 and regained it in the 17th century. It had passed from the Chrichtons to Robert Charteris in 1462 and was sold to James Stewart of Balquhane in 1593.

Fourmerkland Tower

ELSHIESHIELDS   NY 069850

Wilin Johnstone's "house of Elsiechellis" was burnt by Maxwell of Kirkhouse in 1602 and the upper parts of the still inhabited L-plan tower, if not all of it, date from the period immiately afterwards. The wing contains a spiral stair with a bedroom above from which there was access by a ladder up to a watch turret originally furnished with a basket for a beacon fire on top of one of the gables. the other three corners of the main block measuring 8.3m by 7m have round bartizans containing closets opening off the fourth storey which is lighted by dormer windows in the roof. A more modern mansion adjoins the opposite end from the wing.

ENOCH NS 879009

In 1376 Enoch was made into a barony for the Menzies family, owners until the early 18th century. There are foundations of a small late tower beside the Carron Burn.

FOURMERKLAND NX909807

This small tower measuring 7.2m by 5.8m has four storeys, the topmost being partly in the roof and having closets in round bartizans on diagonally opposite corners. Each storey has a single opening in each wall. The tower was inhabited until 1896 and still retains its roof. It bears the date 1590 and the initials of Robert Maxwell and his wife.

FRENCHLAND NT 102054

The French family held land here as tenants of the Bruces in the early 13th century. In the 16th century they built a three storey tower measuring 8m by 6.3m. with a tiny spiral stair squeezed in the SW corner. In the early 17th century Robert French added a turret on the west side to contain a wide stair from a new entrance to the hall and a bedroom at third storey level. It was perhaps at the same time that the main tower was remodelled without the former open wall-walk and parapet. The side walls have mostly fallen but the gables stand intact.

GILLESPIE NY 172919

A road bissects a court 25m long by 20m wide with the much damaged base of a
tower above a steep drop to the river on the east and a rampart and ditch on the other
sides. James Graham was laird here throughout the second and third quarters of the
16th century and probably built the tower.

GILNOCKIE (HOLLOWS) NY 383787

This tower was built c1520 by Johnie Armstrong, a younger brother of the Armstrong
chief Thomas, whose seat was at Mangerton. Johnie was notorious for his lawless
exploits on both sides of the Border and is said to have coined the word blackmail to
describe his extortions. The Armstrongs were said to be able to muster 3,000
horsemen and could not be easily put down but in 1528 the English West March
Warden Sir Christopher Dacre burnt the tower and in 1530 Johnie and 50 followers
were summarily hanged on the spot by James V after being tricked into joining the
King on a hunting party. Only subsequently did the King discover that he had removed
an effective barrier between the Scots and English and left his West March open to
attack. The tower was damaged during the English raids of the 1540s and
subsequently remodelled with a new parapet around an attic with a beacon stance
perched on one gable. The parapet itself is missing there survives the ornamental
corbel-table which supported it and a set of round corner bartizans. A new roof and
floors were provided in the 1970s when the tower was restored and re-occupied by
Johnie's descendant Major Armstrong-Wilson. The tower measures 10m by 7.6m and
has a vaulted cellar with a double splayed gunloop in each wall, a hall above, and two
storeys of private rooms, in addition to the attic already noted. See photo on p14.

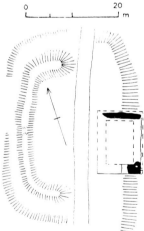

Plan of Gillespie Tower

Glenae Tower

Isle Tower

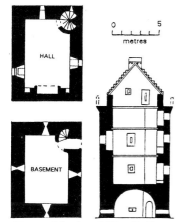

Plans and Section of Gilnockie Tower

Hoddom Castle

GLENAE NX 984905

The lower part of a modest tower lies hidden among trees. A doorway facing east is the only feature. Glenae was held in the early 17th century by Sir John Dalziel, brother of the 2nd Earl of Carnwath, and was made into a barony for his son Robert in 1666.

HODDOM NY 157730

Hoddam belonged to the Herries family of knights who served the Bruces, and then passed to the Carruthers. The massive L-plan tower rise above the River Annan was built by John Maxwell, Lord Herries, soon after he obtained possession in the mid-16th century. It was regarded as a place of some strength but in 1568 an indifferent garrison surrendered the castle to the Regent Moray after a one day siege. He handed it over to Douglas of Drumlanrig to serve as headquarters for the office of Warden of the Scottish West March but in 1569 Hoddom was recaptured by forces loyal to Queen Mary. In 1570 the English commander Lord Scroop captured and blew up the tower. It was restored and after Sir Richard Murray obtained Hoddom from the 6th Lord Herries further remodelling was carried out. Hoddom passed to the Earl of Southesk in 1653, to the Sharp family in 1690, and was later held by the Brooks.

Hoddom Castle now lies derelict on one side of a caravan park. Demolition of a lower later wing has left a scar on the south end wall of the main block which measures 15.5m by 11m and has four storeys and an attic surrounded by a wall-walk 15.3m above ground. The ornamental coursing carrying the parapet and round bartizans continues round a wing 8.7m wide and 22m high. This wing has two full stories above the coursing and ends in a flat roof with an open bartizan at the SE corner, conical roofed bartizans on the west corners, and a higher staircase turret on the NE. Below the foot of the stair is a prison. The entrance doorway has a segmental arch and a bold quirked edge roll moulding with a fillet. The label above the doorway is a big cable with mutilated knotted stops. There is a much altered 17th century courtyard wall on the south and east. Much of the dry moat has now been filled in.

ISLE   NY 028689

A flat site mostly enclosed by a loop of the Lochar Water and said to have had a wet moat on the other side bears the remains of a small three storey tower with a staircase wing in the middle of the NW side. Over the entrance at the foot of this wing was a stone with the year 1622 and the initials of Edward Maxwell and Helen Douglas. A hoarding on stone corbels defended this entrance from above. Most of one end survives, enough to show that the unvaulted basement had double splayed shot-holes.

ISLE   NX 955825

This tower is similar in size, layout, and condition to that at Fourmerkland (p69). the entrance retains a yett and a stone with the year 1587 and the initials of John Fergusson and his wife. Their descemdants later added another block on one corner and a service wing at the other end and were still in possession in the 19th century. The poet Robert Burns is said to have used the tower for a while.

Isle Tower

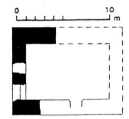

Plan of Langholm Tower

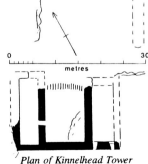

Plan of Kinnelhead Tower

Lag Tower

Langholm Tower

Plan of Lag Tower

Plan of Isle Tower

KINNELHEAD   NT 028017

Two very ruined ranges each about 7.5m wide and 15 and 17m long respectively lie 9m apart. The east range had a vaulted basement partly formed in a natural cleft of one of a number of rock outcrops in the vicinity. A cross incised on native rock nearby suggests the place was originally a monastic cell or grange but it appears to have been subsequently used as a fortified farm steading, there being footings of a thick curtain wall 17m north of the ranges.

LAG   NX 880862

Standing on what looks like a motte is a ruined tower measuring 9m by 7.7m which was probably built by John Grierson who in 1545 was one of the sureties for the captured Robert, Master of Maxwell. A Gilbert Grierson lived here in the early 14th century and another of the same name in 1412 married one of the three heiresses of Sir Duncan Kirkpatrick, lord of Torthorwald. The last occupant is said to have been Sir Robert Grierson, noted for his hostility to the Covenanters. The tower contained four unvaulted storeys but the top-most storey is now destroyed. Part of a barmkin wall and outbuildings still survived in the late 19th century.

LANGHOLM   NY 361849 & 365855

The fragmentary tower 12.6m long by 9m wide near to the confluence of the Esk with the Ewes Water may be the tower betrayed to the English in 1544 and recaptured in 1547 by the Scottish Regent. The cellar of a smaller later tower survives in a wing of the Buccleugh Arms Hotel on the NE side of the main street of the town. Langholm was a Maxwell barony sold to Douglas of Drumlanrig by the 2nd Earl of Nithsdale.

Old print of Lag Tower

LOCHHOUSE NT 082034

The ruined 16th century tower of the Johnstones of Corehead was restored as a residence c1980. it has rounded corners and external offsets below the basement double splayed gunloops and the third storey windows. The attic originall lay inside a vanished parapet for which the corbels remain. The tower measures 11m by 8.3m over walls 1.6m thick at the base. The entrance in the east wall is flanked by a staircase in the corner and a tiny porters room in the side wall. See plan on p85.

LOCHMABEN NY 082822 & 088812

The moated platform 60m in diameter and 6m high on one side of the golf course near the town is the site of the chief Scottish seat of the de Brus Lords of Annandale after the motte at Annan collapsed (see p60.) It is first mentioned in 1173 when temporarily held by William The Lion. It may have had stone buildings by the 13th century. In 1298 Edward I chose a stronger site on a promontory by the loch to the south for a timber fort or peel to help consolidate his hold on Scotland after his victory over Wallace at Falkirk. The peel was strengthened after being besieged by Robert Bruce throughout August 1299 and it was attacked again by 7,000 Scots in 1301. It fell to Bruce in 1306, was recovered, but finally surrendered to the Scots after Bannockburn.

Lochhouse Tower

Lochmaben Motte

From 1333 until 1384, when it was besieged and captured by Archibald the Grim, Lord of Galloway, Lochmaben Castle was in English hands. Edward III had it rebuilt in stone in the 1360s and 70s. Stonework is specifically mentioned in 1365, "cementarios" were among the craftsmen required by the then constable the Bohun Earl of Hereford for repairs in 1373, and two towers were roofed and a drawbridge provided in 1375. The castle was retained by James II after the fall of the Black Douglases in 1455, and in 1542 it was used as a base by James V for mustering forces for his ill-fated campaign ending with the defeat at Solway Moss. From 1410 the Maxwells were hereditary keepers until their rebellion in 1588 when James VI besieged and captured the castle and gave the coveted office of Warden of the West March to their rival the Johnstone Earl of Annandale.

Lochmaben Castle from the SE

Lochmaben Castle from the east

Much stonework standing to a considerable height still remains although there are hardly any surviving features as nearly all the ashlar facing was robbed in the 18th century. It is not easy now to say which parts were roofed and which were open courts either originally or subsequently. It seems that the castle was designed as an open court with wooden buildings against high and unusually thick curtain walls. In front of the landward facing wall in which was the gateway was an ashlar lined canal connecting with the loch and serving as a wet moat. Wing walls with arches over the canal connected with an outer front wall, now destroyed, which had a gateway with twin flanking round towers, perhaps those roofed in 1375. The very thick wall subdividing the court may be associated with the new hall built for James IV c1510. Probably the whole northern half of the court then became a large and massively walled palacial domestic range. At the west end of this part are traces of two vaulted cellars. The walling north of the main court is of uncertain date and purpose. Perhaps it was a service range built for James IV.

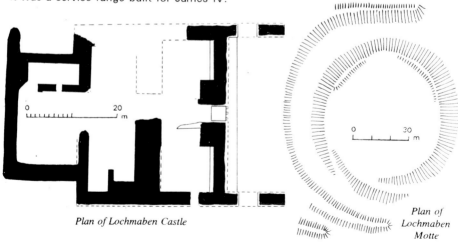

Plan of Lochmaben Castle

Plan of Lochmaben Motte

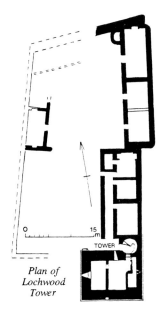

Plan of
Lochwood
Tower

Lochwood Tower

LOCHWOOD NY 085968

The Johnstones were originally knights serving the Bruces. Lochwood was made into a barony for them in 1543, being their chief seat. Titles of Earl of Hartfell and Earl of Annandale were granted in 1643 and the 1660s. The big L-plan tower with a wide spiral staircase and entrance in the wing, and a prison in the thickness of the adjoining end wall was built c1500. Only one corner stands above the cellar vaults. Beyond the wing is a range with two cellars and kitchen connected by a corridor. This may have existed by 1547 when the castle was captured by the English having been "kept only with two or three fellows and as many wenches" and was said to then have a "barnkin, hall, kitchen, and stalles". Later on the barmkin was extended further north to the foot of the still surviving tree-clad 12th century motte which dominates the court and would have made it untenable against a force holding the motte summit, an odd weakness. The wall facing the mound was thick and seems to have contained a gateway although the main entrance probably remained on the south beside the tower. The extension has a second range on the east side out of axis with the earlier one. The walls of these ranges stand in a featureless and somewhat rebuilt state about 2m high with a cement capping. In 1585 the Maxwell-Johnstone feud reached a climax with the burning of Lochwood by Robert Maxwell and the Armstrongs, all the early Johnstone charters being lost. The castle was abandoned after another fire in 1710.

LOCKERBIE NY 136816

In 1585 the towers of Andrew and Mungo Johnstone at Lockerbie were besieged and captured by the Earl of Morton. Mungo Johnstone's tower withstood another attack in 1593 when Lord Maxwell attempted to capture and destroy it. The Johnstone chief came to the rescue and Lord Maxwell was defeated and slain. One of the towers remained until a few years ago by the main street. It measured just 7.5m by 6m and had rounded corners and renewed windows. There were four corbels from the parapet reset when the building was reduced to two storeys. There were two cellars with vaults running in opposite directions. The tower was at one time used as the town jail.

LUNELLY   NY 193821

Just a fragment 7m high and 6m long remains of the south wall of this tower probably built by James Johnstone after he obtained Lunelly from Lord Maxwell in 1516.

MAXWELLTON   NS 822898

This house dated 1641 bears an inscription in Latin meaning "unless The Lord assist your undertakings in vain you erect proud buildings", plus the arms and initials of John Lawrie and Agnes Grierson. John had recently obtained the property from the the the Maxwell Earl of Glencairn. A secondary entrance facing the conservatory has over it a shield and a cartouche bearing the names of Sir Robert Lawrie and Dame Jean Riddell. The Lawries lived here until the house was sold and restored in the 1960s.

MELLINGSHAW   NT 038087

Of this 16th century Johnstone tower by a burn only a 4.5m high fragment of a corner containing the spiral staircase with one jamb of the adjacent doorway now survives.

MORTON   NX 891992

The fine defensive site on a promontory above a small artificial loch was occupied by an early castle destroyed in 1357. The barony was held by Thomas Randolph during Robert Bruce's reign although the castle was then presumably in a dismantled state like the other neighbouring fortresses. It passed to the Earl of March who built the existing structure and in 1459 was given by James II to James Douglas of Dalkeith, later created Earl of Morton after the place of that name he held in Lothian. No walls now remain on the stronger two sides of the triangular court 30m by 40m but towards the flat approach is a very long two storey block which contained a hall over a basement which was subdivided into a series of rooms for storing and preparing food and drink. At the east end of the hall was a private room with a smaller room opening off it in a round corner tower. The main lordly apartments, however, were probably contained in the gatehouse at the west end, where a passageway was flanked by a pair of D-shaped towers, one of which stands four storeys high. The passage was closed by a portcullis and was approached by a ramp and turning bridge over a pit.

MOUSEWALD   NY 051739

Close to Mousewald Place is a 9m high fragment of a tower with an unvaulted cellar. Mousewald passed by marriage from the Carruthers' family to Douglas of Drumlanrig.

Morton Castle

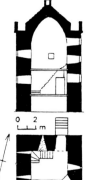

Repentance Tower

Robgill Tower

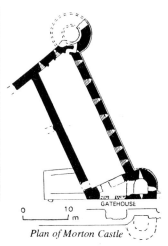

GATEHOUSE

0   10
|_____| m

Plan of Morton Castle

OLD CRAWFORDTON NX 815889

The basement of a late 16th century tower 10m long by 5.8m wide adjoins a farm building. A passage connects the entrance in the middle of the north wall to two vaulted cellars and the foot of the staircase in the NW corner. Old Crawfordton was held by John Chrichton in 1656.

PORTRACK NX 935832

Near Portrack House is a 4m high and 2.5m long fragment of walling 1.2m thick of a Maxwell tower by the River Nith. A stream defends the site on the north and east and there was a ditch to the south and west.

RAECLEUGH NT 038118

Near a farm are the last remnants of a Johnstone tower 11m long by 6.5m wide with roughly built walls ranging in thickness from 0.9m to 1.5m.

REPENTANCE NY 155723

On a hill commanding extensive southward views near Hoddom Castle is a small tower built in the 1560s by John Maxwell, Lord Herries, as a lookout, signalling post, and commemorative folly. He perhaps sought forgiveness for past misdeeds, hence the word Repentance over the doorway leading into the middle of three dark storeys without fireplaces or latrines. From the doorway wooden stairs within the rooms lead up to the third storey and the wall-walk with a plain parapet around a roof in the form of a vault covered with flagstones making the tower virtually fireproof. Perched on the top is a stance for a beacon fire. The tower was never permanently lived in.

ROBGILL NY 248716

This tower was probably built by Cuthbert Irvine, one of many local lairds obliged by force to support the English Crown in 1547. It had then been recently burnt by the English Warden of the West March, Lord Wharton. The tower remained complete until the late 19th century when the upper storeys were removed and a new dining room and bedrooms serving a later adjacent mansion were grafted onto the old basement then divided but originally forming a kitchen with a fireplace in the west end wall. The entrance lobby lies beside the staircase in the SE corner and has a built up hatch in the ceiling in which has been placed a pendant carved with the monogram I.H.S.

ROCKHALL   NY 054754

One wing of the much altered L-plan building overlooking Solway Firth retains original late 16th century slit windows in its vaulted basement. The other wing is 17th century. This was a Grierson seat since the 15th century. It is said to be haunted by the pet monkey of Sir Robert Grierson, a notorious persecutor of Covenanters, and animal having been slain by servants after Sir Robert's death.

SANQUHAR   NS 795093

The Chrichtons obtained Sanquhar by marrying a Ross heiress in the early 14th century. They increased their estates after the fall of the Black Douglases in 1455 and in 1485 gained a peerage as Lords Chrichton of Sanquhar. The four storey ashlar faced tower 7m square at the south corner is all that remains of what was probably intended as a courtyard castle of c1380 with similar towers at the other corners. The design may have been changed before completion as by c1400 a hall block of which little remains had been built on the NE side of the court. In keeping with the rise in family prosperity a new wing with a gateway passage flanked by rectangular rooms was added on the NW side. The room north of the passage was a guardroom with a sleeping loft above, whilst that on the south contained a well and lay within a half round tower 9m in diameter flanking the gate. Above was a hall with a private room in the round tower forming a private suite for the lord. The latter has its own staircase down to the court. On the SW side of the court are very ruined service rooms of the late 16th century. The round stair turret between the old hall and guard room, the wall connecting the old hall to the south tower, and the wall of the outer court to the NW, all now reduced to their foundations, date from about the time when William Chrichton entertained James VI at Sanquhar in 1617. He was created Earl of Dumfries by Charles I in 1633 but the barony was sold in 1639 to Sir William Douglas of Drumlanrig, later 1st Earl of Queensberry. After the 1st Duke of Queensberry died in 1700 his son the 2nd Duke transferred his seat to the splendid new mansion that his father had built at Drumlanrig and Sanquhar was left to decay.

Spedlins Tower

SPEDLINS   NY 098877

The Jardines had their seat here by the late 12th century. The massive two lower storeys of the tower are clearly 15th century work whilst the stone with the year 1605 refers to the rebuilding of the two upper storeys with thinner walling allowing an arrangement of two rooms on either side of a central corridor. There are twin gables at each end with conical roofed bartizans. The splendid hall fireplace also goes with the new work. A prison in the older part is reached by a hatch from the upper lobby of the stairs from the entrance to the hall. The tower eventually became a ruin after the Jardines built a new mansion nearby but was re-roofed in the 1960s.

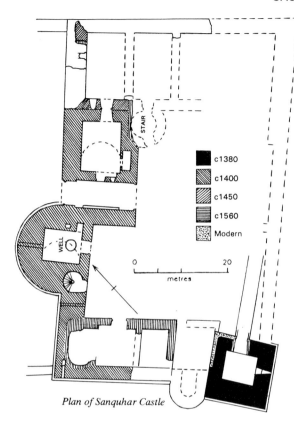

c1380
c1400
c1450
c1560
Modern

0   20
metres

Plan of Sanquhar Castle

Corner Tower, Sanquhar

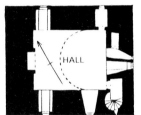

HALL

Plan of Spedlins Tower

Gatehouse, Sanquhar

Stapleton Tower

STAPLETON   NY 234688

This tower 13m long by 8.3 wide was built in the 16th century by the Irvines. The shell of the three storeys over a vaulted basement with a spiral stair in the east corner remains fairly complete. It has had a number of minor alterations made to it over the years and bears the scars of the recently demolished mansion which adjoined the north wall. The cellar originally had a shot-hole in each wall but now has two medium sized windows in place of two of them, a fireplace blocking a third, and a fourth closed up. Fergus Graham of Blacketwood was residing in the tower when Christie Irvine, who considered himself to have rights over the estate, captured the place in a surprise early morning attack in January 1626. The local gentry were ordered to eject Irvine and his men who were still in possession in July although the outcome is not recorded.

SUNDAYWELL   NX 811845

Parts of a 16th century tower remain in the farmhouse. A reset stone dated 1651 bears the initials of James Kirkoe and his wife Susan Walsh of Colliston.

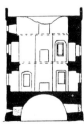

Plans and Section of Stapleton Tower

TIBBERS NX 863983

Hidden among woods on a promontory in the Drumlanrig estate are the very ruined and overgrown remnants of a stone castle begun in 1298 on an older motte by Sir Richard Siward, Sheriff of Dumfries, a Scot who sided with Edward I. The English king visited the castle in September that year after his victory at Falkirk and he gave £100 towards the work in 1302. The garrison in 1300 numbered 21 including eight archers. The castle was captured by Bruce's forces in 1306 but was quickly retaken by the English who hanged John de Seton who had been left in charge of it. During that summer it was garrisoned with 50 archers and 11 squires. Tibbers later passed to the Dunbar Earls of March and then to the Maitlands of Auchen although it is likely that the castle was dismantled after the English defeat at Bannockburn and not used again. A rampart and ditch close off a spacious bailey to the south. Walls 2.3m thick nowhere more than 3.5m high enclose a court 31m long with a greatest width of 21m with a hall with another block in front in the NW corner, another block in the SW corner and a well near the middle. There were round towers 7m in diameter at each corner with the gateway beside that on the SE. There are footings for a fifth tower on the south side on the other side of the gateway but it appears to have been never completed or not restored after being slighted as the curtain wall continues unbroken across its site. There are foundations of a barbican which took the form of walls flanking a drawbridge or turning bridge. The east curtain wall took the odd form of two thin parallel walls with a space between. Because of the resulting greater thickness the corner towers hardly projected beyond the outermost face. Close to the NE tower there was a dog-leg shaped postern through this system of walls.

TORTHORWALD   NY 033783

A family of knights called the de Torthorwalds created the rectangular moated platform in the 13th century. The much ruined tower with some parts patched to prevent their collapse which lies on the west side of the platform was probably built c1360-1400 by their successors the Carlyles who were created peers c1475. Sir James Douglas of Parkhead married a Carlyle heiress in 1609 and in 1621 Torthorwald passed to the Douglases of Drumlanrig, late Dukes of Queensberry. The tower measures 17m by 12, but has a straight joint on the east side and thinner and cruder walling at the north end suggesting that whilst the pointed upper vault over the hall was under construction it was enlarged to the present dimensions. Below the hall were a cellar and sleeping loft under a round vault and above was a more thinly walled apartment for the lord now reduced to just a fragment perhaps of later date. Ragged holes remain of the hall fireplace and nearby side windows plus a spiral stair from the sleeping loft to the roof in the SW corner. A second stair in the NE corner connected only the loft and the hall. There are indications that the original entrance was at loft level in the east wall as at the contemporary tower at Threave, but in the modified plan a new ground level entrance was provided in the north wall.

WAMPHRAY   NY 130965

Foundations remain near the confluence of the Lemoir Burn and the Wamphray Water. John Johnstone was imprisoned in his own home for his part in the 1745 rebellion. He avoided execution by escaping after changing places with a kinsman.

WESTERHALL   NS 320893

This Johnstone seat has a small court containing a tower-like building with a round angle turret in one corner and on the opposite side is a range which is thought to have been reduced from three storeys to two. There is some fine 18th century panelling.

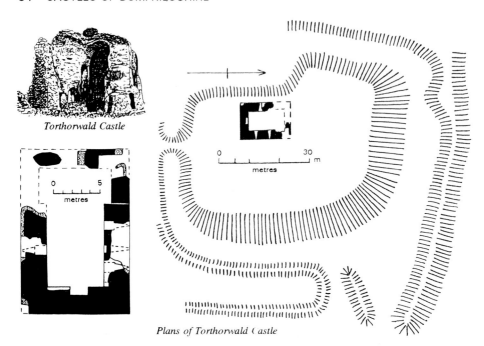

Torthorwald Castle

Plans of Torthorwald Castle

WOODHOUSE NY 251715

Much of this 16th century Irvine tower collapsed in the 19th century so only the north wall with the NE corner containing the staircase entirely rebuilt still stands up to the height of the parapet corbelling. The entrance did not adjoin the stair but was probably at the east end of the south wall despite the present gap being at the west end. The basement retains two double splayed gunports and there was a vaulted sleeping loft above. Parts of the hall and bedroom fireplaces remain in the west end wall stump.

Woodhouse Tower

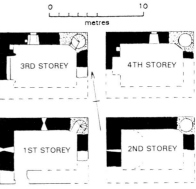

3RD STOREY

4TH STOREY

1ST STOREY

2ND STOREY

Plans of Woodhouse Tower

LIST OF EARTHWORKS

APPLEGARTH NY 104842 32m diameter platform above east bank of the Annan.

AULDTON A.M. NT 094058 Ditched mound 8m high with with rectangular bailey 60m by 48m to the south and south-west. Formerly protected by marshland. See p6.

BALLAGGAN NS 835014 Small mound with further outer slopes to NE and NW. p6.

BIRKSHAW NX 865857 Mound on flattish site 1km north of Dunscore Village.

BURRANCE NY 095858 Moated site. Predecessor of Spedlins Tower 2km to N.

CARRONGLEN NS 886038 Nearly rectangular moated platform on flattish site.

COATS HILL NT 073042 4m high oval mound on hill 1km NE of Auchan Castle. p6.

COURANCE HILL NY 045914 Earthwork on flattish site at north end of lake.

CRAWSTON NX 895858 Small mound on the east slope of Crawston Hill.

DINNING NX 892901 Promontory made into a small mound with a pair of 22m wide baileys extending in line for 67m to the SE with a ditch between them. p6.

DRUIDHILL NS 810014 Mound in a remote site by Cairn and Druidhill burns.

DUNCOW NX 975843 Mound on hill 0.7km NE of village.

ENOCH NS 878007 Mound and bailey in woods above Carron Burn and tributary.

GARPOL WATER NT 051049 3m high mound with bailey to north and burn to south.

HUTTON NY 163894 8m high ditched mound and outworks on an elevated site. p6.

INGLESTON NX 799900 Mound and bailey on south side of Cairn Water.

MALLS CASTLE NY 150796 Earthworks between railway and the Water of Milk.

MAXWELLTON NX 818897 Mound in woodland east of the Cairn water.

ROCKHILL NY 055767 Ditched mound 5m high with small bailey to NE. Plan p6.

RYEHILL NS 794086 Platform of irregular shape on above Nith near Sanquhar.

TINWALD NY 003815 Mound above stream to south of church in village.

WAMPHRAY NY 128966 Mound and bailey near site of tower by Wamphray Water.

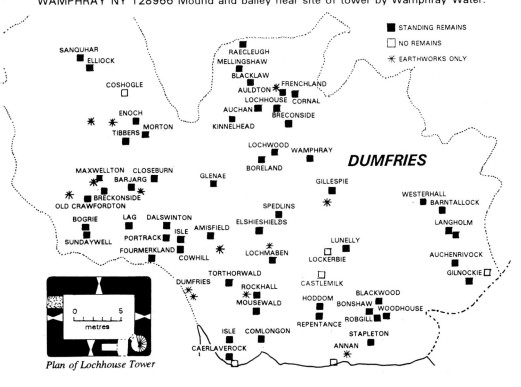

Plan of Lochhouse Tower

GAZETTEER OF CASTLES IN GALLOWAY

ABBOT'S TOWER   NX 972666

This building was in a very poor state until restoration began recently. It was abandoned c1790 and the cellar was choked with vegetation and rubble from its collapsed vault. The tower lies at the foot of a steep slope below a hill crest 1km NE of Sweetheart Abbey. It was built c1560 by the penultimate abbot, John Brown, a junior member of the Carsluith Browns. The tower measures 8.9m by 7.2m and is built of granite boulders with much smaller stones in between. The hall has a fireplace in the east wall, a latrine in the SW corner and a window in each other wall. There are two upper storeys with fireplaces in the west wall, the topmost being an attic with a bartizan on one corner and a projecting caphouse over the staircase in the wing.

AUCHENSKEOCH   NX 917588

In the steading of Castle Farm is a ruined tower 5m in diameter and an adjacent length of walling 11.2m long by 0.8m thick which probably date from the late 16th century. The tower contains an irregularly shaped living room with a blocked up fireplace and two small windows over a round basement with three gunports, two of which flanked the adjacent walls. Both it and the adjacent walling which has three upper storey windows with holes for iron bars stand to the original height of about 6m. Either this castle took the unusual form of a two storey mansion around an open court or the surviving fragments were part of the court and outbuildings of a lost tower house.

AUCHNESS   NX 106447

This still inhabited building is a tower of c1600 which has been extended and altered. It was a jointure house of the McDoualls and measures about 6m square with walls 0.9m thick and has no vaults. The bartizans on the tops of the corners are not ancient.

BALDOON   NX 426536

Baldoon passed in the 1530s to Archibald Dunbar, son of Sir John Dunbar of Westfield, whose descendants held it until c1800. By a farm is a wall 19m long, 7.5m high and 1m thick remaining from a plain unfortified 17th century mansion. Several windows and a doorway remain. Between this wall and the farmhouse are a fine pair of Baroque gateposts of c1700.

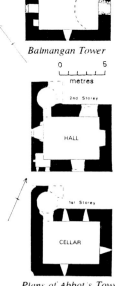

Balmangan Tower

0   5

metres

2nd Storey

HALL

1st Storey

CELLAR

Plans of Abbot's Tower

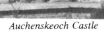

Auchenskeoch Castle

Abbot's Tower

Auchness Castle

Baldoon Castle

Balmangan Tower

BALMANGAN   NX 651456

In the garden of a house opposite Balmangan Farm is the ivy mantled vaulted basement of a 16th century tower measuring 9.3m by 6.9m. The entrance lay close to the now inaccessible staircase in the north corner. The only original loop lighting the cellar has a roundel at top and bottom. There are also two recesses. Only the lowest courses survive of the hall above the vault, without any features remaining.

BALZIELAND   NX 097428

Incorporated in the garden wall of Logan House is a fragment 1.2m thick and two storeys high of a 16th century tower house of the McDoualls of Logan.

BARCLOSH   NX 855624

By a farm is a 3.5m high fragment of half the south end wall with the jamb of a window embrasure of a small 16th century tower 6.6m wide over walls 1.2m thick.

BARHOLM   NX 521529

The M'Cullochs acquired Barholm c1510 and erected the tower standing 100m above the sea about fifty years later. The building is much obscured with vegetation and ivy and is only visible at close quarters from an adjacent track on the other side of which is a ravine separating it from a steeply rising hillside. The tower measures 10.6m by 7.8m over walls 1.6m thick below the cellar vault. The hall fireplace in a side wall between two windows has been reduced in width at a later date. Above was the laird's suite of two rooms. The servants' room was mostly in the roof and was surrounded by an open wall-walk. At this level the wing containing the main staircase is widened into a two storey caphouse served by a stair corbelled out over the re-entrant angle, the upper room having a vault supporting an open look-out post formerly with a parapet. Two of the main staircase windows have roll mouldings and decoratively shaped heads and the segmental arched doorway at the foot of the stair has an outer cable moulding which is tied in a knot at each end and has somewhat haphazardly arranged on it two masks and an animal.

BARSCOBE   NX 660806

This is a still inhabited unfortified L-planned laird's house bearing over the doorway and top windows the date 1648 and the initials of William Maclellan of Bombie and his wife who was either Mary, daughter of Sir Robert Gordon of Lochinvar or Margaret, daughter of John Gordon of Airds. The house has a lofty room with attractive dormer windows lighting the third storey and has only occasional crowsteps instead on a continuous series. Robert Maclellan, laird of Barscobe from 1664 was a prominent Covenanter. His descendants remained in possession until 1799.

BOMBIE   NX 708502

West of the present house are slight traces of a moated site lacking any traces of stone buildings. This was the seat of the Maclellans until they took up residence in the burgh of Kirkcudbright in the 16th century.

The entrance doorway, Barholm

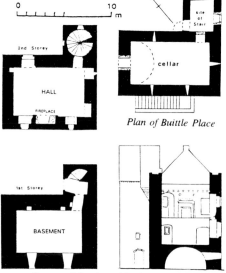

Plan of Buittle Place

Plans and Section of Barholm Castle

Buittle Place

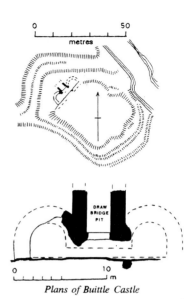

Plans of Buittle Castle

BUITTLE   NX 819616 & 817617

Dervorguilla of Galloway and her husband John Balliol are thought to have built a stone castle here beside the Water of Urr in the 1240s, possibly on the site of a former timber structure. It superseded the Mote of Urr further upstream at the chief stronghold of eastern Kirkcudbright. Dervorguilla remained in residence at Buittle until her death in 1290 as her son, who succeeded his father in 1267, had extensive northern English estates centred on Barnard Castle to preoccupy him. In 1292 he was chosen by Edward I of England as his puppet King of Scotland. Buittle was returned to him after having been kept for a while by the Bruces, but it was occupied by English forces from the time of John's deposition by Edward in 1296 until the Bruces captured and destroyed it c1313. Edward Balliol may have briefly re-occupied the site in the 1330s when he was ruling Scotland but the site shows no evidence of later repairs.

The castle comprises a courtyard roughly 30m square with a surrounding ditch filled from the adjacent river. The site is overgrown and tree covered and all that remains of stonework is some crumbling corework below courtyard level facing the river and parts of a gatehouse occupying most of the NW side. The most impressive relic is a drawbridge pit 2.7m wide and 3.5m deep built of fine sandstone ashlar faced walls 1.6m thick. On either side of the passage behind were round fronted towers 8m in diameter with walls about 2m thick. These had basement rooms below courtyard level connected by a passage below the main entrance passageway.

In the late 16th century an L-plan tower called Buittle Place was built higher up to the west. It became a ruin in the 18th century but was restored and now serves as a farmhouse. It measures 11.2m by 6.9m and contains a single vaulted cellar with four narrow slit windows. The hall is now divided into three rooms and its fireplace in a side wall is blocked up. It is now reached by an external stair although the original access was by a stair in a square well in the wing with the entrance at its foot. Only a few bottom treads survive of the secondary staircase over the re-entrant angle and the round bartizans containing closets at attic level have been entirely removed.

CALLY   NX 598554

NW of the hotel and below the west side of the loch is one end wall of a 16th century tower 7.1m wide. It is 1.2m thick and now only 4m high. There were four storeys.

CARDONESS   A.M.*   NX 591552

The McCullochs acquired Cardoness c1450 and built this impressive tower on a rock by the Water of Fleet between then and 1500. They were noted law-breakers, the second laird and probably builder of the tower being outlawed in 1471 and 1480. In 1690 Sir Geoffrey McCulloch shot Gordon of Bush O'Bield at his own front door and was subsequently executed when he returned from exile abroad. Cardoness passed to the Gordons and later to the Maxwells. It is now maintained by the State.

The knob of rock on which the tower stands has been extended to the south and west by adding on cellars in each direction. Any structures which may have stood above these have gone leaving the tower now effectively surrounded by a platform 3m high with railings instead of a parapet. The platform is reached by a ramp up from a small level court with the cellars forming two sides and foundations of other buildings on the other sides, which are those naturally protected by the cliffs above the estuary. The arrangement suggests that cannon covering the estuary may have been mounted at one time, thus necessitating a ramp rather than steps, and being able to shoot out over the low courtyard buildings. The approach path from the NE led to an outer gate giving onto a narrow and irregularly shaped outer court around the east side.

In the British Museum is a late 16th century report on Cardoness when the English were considering the possible advantages of occupying the tower for strategic reasons. The report comments on the difficulty of battering this strongpoint with cannon either by sea or land. It is described as lacking a barmkin or battlements. The court is quite likely to have been an addition made after the time of the report. The second comment is more difficult to reconcile with the remains as the tower had an open wall-walk and parapet as first built. New end gables flush with the outer wall replaced these at each end but the side walls still bear open wall-walks now lacking their parapets. At that time small ships could anchor directly below the cliffs.

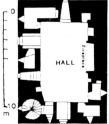

Cardoness Tower   *Plans of Cardoness Tower*

Cardoness Tower measures 13.1m by 9.7m and rises 16m to the wall-walks. There were six storeys in all as below the vault supporting the hall floor were not only two cellars at ground level but a low sleeping loft above. The round headed doorway has a draw-bar slot and leads into a lobby commanded by a murder hole from a small room above. Off the lobby are doorways to a small guard room, the spiral stair, the small wine cellar, and the larger food cellar with round recesses at the far end possibly for grain storage. At loft level the end wall beside the stair contains a prison with a latrine. A hatch in the floor gives onto a dungeon pit below. The hall is provided with several good windows and mural rooms and has a fine ogival headed aumbry alongside the remains of a large and fine fireplace. An arch supports a wall dividing the laird's suite on the fourth storey and the two bedrooms above instead of the usual timber partition. The sixth storey was an attic in the roof.

CARSCREUGH   NX 224599

Carscreugh originally belonged to Glenluce Abbey and in the early 17th century was sold by the Vaus family of Barndarroch to the Rosses of Balneil. The existing thinly walled ruin 20m long with square wings at either end of the now mostly destroyed NW side was built c1680 for James Dalrymple, Lord Stair, who had married Margaret, heiress of James Ross in 1665, but it likely there was an older house on the site.

CARSLUITH   A.M. NX 495542

This ruin lies in a farmyard overlooking the sea. A pond or moat formerly separated it from the coast road. Carsluith belonged to the Cairns family until 1460 when it went to James Lindsey. The tower is thought to have been built soon after the estate passed to the Browns after Sir Herbert Lindsey was killed at Flodden in 1513. The Browns remained catholic during the 16th century and were in a perpetual state of feud with the protestant McCullochs of neighbouring Barholm. In 1579 John Brown was fined £40 when his namesake son failed to appear to answer charges on murdering the laird of Barholm. The tower was left to decay after the Browns emigrated to India in 1748.

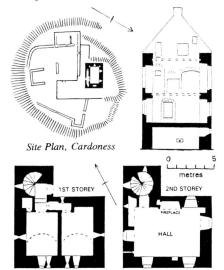

Site Plan, Cardoness

Plans and Section of Carsluith Castle

Carsluith Castle

The main block of the tower at Carsluith measures 9.8m by 7.6. and is 10m high to the eaves. The two vaulted cellars have lighting slits and double splayed gunloops. The hall above has five windows and a fireplace in the north wall. Above were two bedrooms. Level with the attic are sections of open wall-walk on the end walls with corner roundels and the wing is widened on corbelling to provide a third bedroom. The date 1564 with the Brown arms and initial in a niche over the entrance probably record the time when the wing was added. Various cubbyholes in the adjoining part of the main block may be relics of an original narrow staircase in the corner. An unusual feature of the tower was the balcony at third storey level reached from the stair by a doorway now blocked up and leading to the furthest room of the laird's suite.

CASSENCARIE   NX 476577

A much altered and extended early 17th century building lies in ruins above the coast road south of Creetown. See photograph on page 121.

CASTLE FEATHER   NX 447343

A promontory with cliffs up to 30m above the sea has a series of ditches to landward, one of which has a wall face on the inner side. Within them are footings of a tower.

CASTLE KENNEDY   A.M.   NX 111609

The White Loch and the Black Loch were originally one lake with the castle on an island in the middle as shown on Grose's engraving of 1789. John, Lord Kennedy was appointed keeper by James IV of a castle here in 1482 but the existing building was erected in the 1600s for the 5th Earl of Cassilis. It passed from the Kennedys to Sir John Dalrymple, later Viscount Stair, in the late 17th century and has been a ruin since being accidentally burnt in 1716. It lies in ornamental grounds open to the public. The castle consists of a lofty tower house with lower two storey buildings adjoining to the north and west. The north range is clearly an addition of Lord Stair's time but the other part is bonded to and probably contemporary with the main block. Square towers flank the east side facing the approach in which is the entrance which gives onto a passage connecting several vaulted cellars. In the western re-entrant angles behind the towers are square six storey towers one of which contained a staircase leading off the passage. Above the vaults were a hall then three upper storeys of what were probably suites with tower bedrooms opening off day rooms in the main block. See plan p16.

Castle Kennedy

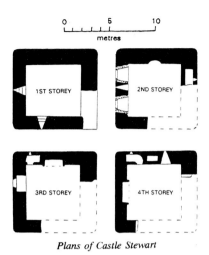

Plans of Castle Stewart

Castle Stewart

CASTLE STEWART NX 379691

This building is named after Colonel William Stewart who made a fortune fighting abroad under Gustavus Adolphus of Sweden and returned to but the estate here previously known as Calcruchie. He is claimed as the builder but the tower looks more like a building of about a century earlier. It stands east of a stream and originally had beyond it a small court containing a kitchen and other outbuildings. Fragments of these survived until c1900 but a modern house has now replaced them. The rough rubble built tower with rounded corners measures 9.1m by 8.6m and is 12m high to the corbels of the destroyed parapet. There were four unvaulted storeys plus an attic in the roof. The walls are mostly 1.4m thick except on the east where a destroyed corner is assumed to have contained the stairs and tiny mural chambers. What was originally a dark servants' hall on the second storey was later given two large west windows without the iron bars which were filled in the window above them. The third and fourth storey rooms formed the laird's suite and have latrines in the NW corner and fireplaces in the north and west walls respectively.

CASTLE WIGG NX 431430

Hidden away among trees and shrubs in an estate and not easy to find is a large ruined ivy-clad mansion in one corner of which is a tower having over the entrance a shield with the date 1593 and the initials of Archibald Stewart of Bardye and Tonderghie and his wife, a member of the M'Kerlie family. Archibald was a kinsman of Stewart of Garlies and had purchased the estate of Wigg from Sir John Vaus in 1584. The tower measures 9.7m by 6.6m with walls 1.1m thick. The entrance is finely moulded and has two checks for a yett and wooden door respectively. It leads into a lobby with doorways into two vaulted cellars. It appears that originally there was also a staircase contained in a round turret opening off the lobby and that there was a second stair in a turret corbelled out at the diagonally opposite corner at the level of the hall to give direct access to the bedrooms at that end. In the 17th century the tower was made into an L-plan by adding a wing without vaults to the southern half of the west side. This wing was later lengthened, and then the mansion added.

CLANYARD   NX 109374

Only a small fragment of what appears to have been a wing containing a scale-and-platt staircase of an L-plan tower of c1600-20 survives of the building described by Symson in 1684 as "a very great house pertaining to Gordon of Clanyard, but it is now something ruinous". On the nearby hill to the SW is a possible overgrown motte.

CORRA   NX 867662

Only one gable 7.1m wide and part of a side wall remain of a building of two storeys and an attic which was probably similar to that at Edingham but without any vaulting.

CORSEWALL   NX 991715

The lands of Corsewall are mentioned in a charter of David II as being the property of Sir Alan Stewart of Dreghorn who was the ancestor of the Darnley Stewarts. Little remains above the basement of 15th century tower 12.8m long by by 10.2m wide over walls 2.4m thick above a plinth which has been mostly ripped away. There are two loops, a rough hole of the doorway with the base of the stair beside it, a shoot from an upper storey latrine, and a hatch in the vault for hoisting supplies. Symson in 1684 calls Corsewall "a considerable house, but now wholly ruinous".

Plans of Craigcaffie Castle

Corsewall Castle

Clanyard Castle

CRAIGCAFFIE   NX 089641

This derelict building lying in a field measures 9.4m by 6m and bears the date 157- on a gable skewput and in a panel high over the entrance are the arms and initials of John Neilson and Margaret Strang. Robert Bruce granted Craigcaffie to his illegitimate son Neil, Earl of Carrick, from whom the Neilsons were descended. They held the tower until it passed to the Earl of Stair in 1791. A wide stair connecting the four storeys occupies half of the width of the building. The remaining width at this end is used to contain small chambers so the three lowest main rooms are nearly square. The vaulted basement seems to have been a kitchen as it has a well (not filled in) and a fireplace. Above was the hall and the third storey was the laird's suite with the bed in the smaller room beside the stair. The fourth storey was an attic with a machicolation corbelled out over the entrance and doorways at either end opening onto sections of wall-walk with parapets and corner roundels with shotholes carried on several corbelled courses. The wall-walks are drained by means of gargoyles.

CRAIGLAW   NX 305611

Within the modern mansion is the vaulted cellar of a tower house with rounded external corners and walls 1.6m to 2.2m thick. The entrance lies hidden inside the later works and has a passage from to an adjacent spiral stair. Within the hall of the present house are two stones. The one dated 1644 must refer to an alteration or addition. The other may refer to the construction of the tower as it has the arms of William Gordon and his wife, one of the Baillies of Lamington. William was given the lands in 1500 by his father William after their recent purchase from Andrew Muir.

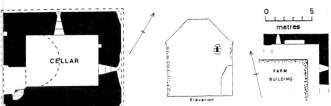
Plan of Corsewall Castle

Plan and Elevation of Corra Castle

Castle Stewart

Craigcaffie Tower

Cruggleton Castle

CRUGGLETON   NX 484428

In the 12th century the early Lords of Galloway had a wooden castle comprising a motte above a vertical sea cliff with a bailey, now only defined by a shallow ditch, to landward. A wall 2.4m to 3m thick around a court roughly 24m square on top of the motte was built either in the 1230s by Earl Alan, or more probably by his daughter Alena and her husband the Earl of Winchester after the native rebellion of 1247 against the Normans and English. Of it there remain only the south corner about 1.2m high and some massive but confused foundations on the north. The castle passed to Alexander Comyn, Earl of Buchan, and Sheriff of Wigtown from 1264 until his death in 1289. In 1292 his son was licensed by Edward I of England to take lead from ruins on the Calf of Man to cover eight of the towers of the castle. This statement is hard to reconcile with the what is known of the structure on the motte which at that time appears to have been a towerless walled enclosure with lean-to domestic ranges of timber. Perhaps the towers were wooden ones flanking the bailey palisade.

The Comyns lost their English lands for supporting John Balliol in 1296 and later had their Scottish estates taken from them by Robert Bruce. The latter made his brother Edward Lord of Galloway in 1308 and Cruggleton was presumably one of the thirteen castles in the province which had to be captured before Edward could rule there. It was presumably destroyed a few years afterwards. Cruggleton was granted to Lord Soulis who gave part of the estate to Whithorn Priory, but the castle site seems to have gone to the Douglases and the tower house about 15m square which lay within the west corner of the court was perhaps built c1370-80 by Archibald the Grim, Lord of Galloway. It had a thick crosswall carrying the vaults of two cellars. Most of the southern cellar survives except for the south corner which has fallen along with the cliff at this point. Just a fragment supported on an iron frame remains of the vault. The other cellar has vanished and was later replaced by a thinly walled outbuilding. When and how this tower house was destroyed it uncertain. Perhaps it was slighted by James II when he defeated the Douglases in 1455. See photo on p95.

By the late 16th century the castle had been rebuilt and the base of the 6m square east tower dates from then. In c1573 the Regent Moray was asked for help by Robert Stewart, the Commendator or lay Abbot of Whithorn Priory, who was then being besieged in Cruggleton Castle by John, 5th Lord Flemming who was trying to enforce his own claim to it. In 1579 the Privy Council ordered that the castle was to be given to Margaret Stewart, widow of Andro Stewart, to whom it was feued by the Commendator. It appears that this order was enforced only when the Commendator himself and Stewart of Garlies captured Cruggleton in a surprise night attack. In 1591 the castle was occupied by James Kennedy for whom Stewart of Garlies was making things difficult. In 1613 James Kennedy of Cruggleton was denounced as a rebel but got off free because the charge was wrongly addressed after he seized Alexander Myrtoun and imprisoned him in the castle dungeon. Kennedy later got into debt and in 1620 Cruggleton was transferred to Andrew Agnew of Lochnaw. It had been mostly demolished for its materials by the time Symson saw the site in the 1680s. In 1978-82 the castle site, which lies isolated far from any road east of the Norman church, was excavated. The motte top was almost stripped bare but not much was found either in the way of wall bases or artifacts, and the site is growing over again.

CULLOCHAN   NX 920755

Slight traces remain of a 16th century tower measuring 11m by 6.3m. They lie on the partly lowered pear-shaped summit measuring 27m by 19m of a motte created out of a spur high above the Cargen Water but cutting a 3m deep ditch to landward. The site is covered with trees and is difficult to reach.

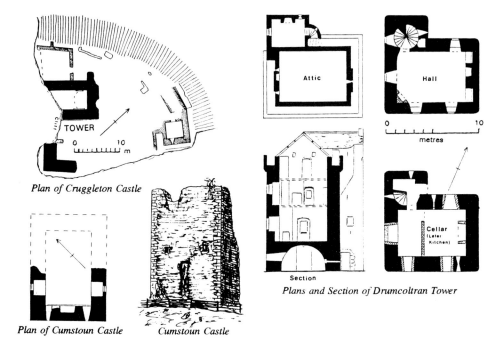

Plan of Cruggleton Castle

Plan of Cumstoun Castle   *Cumstoun Castle*

Plans and Section of Drumcoltran Tower

CUMSTOUN NX 683533

The SW half of a 16th century tower 11.3m by 8.4m stands on a mound Sw of the modern mansion overlooking the Dee estuary. Neither the cellar nor the servant's hall-cum-kitchen above with large later windows were vaulted. The hall on the third storey had a fireplace in the end wall flanked by small windows high up, and there were the usual side windows. There were bedrooms on the fourth storey and at least one more habitable level in the roof. The entrance and staircase lay in the destroyed half.

DRUMCOLTRAN A.M. NX 869684

Drumcoltran belonged to the Harries family from 1368 until 1550 when Sir John Maxwell, second son of Lord Maxwell married Agnes, co-heiress of Lord Herries of Terregles. The tower may date from c1550-60 but could be slightly earlier. In 1168 it passed to the Irvings. It subsequently went to the Hynds and Herons and then in 1845 reverted to the Maxwells of Terregles. It is now maintained by the State. The tower measures 10.2m by 8m above a slightly battered base and is 12.5m high to the top of the parapet protecting the wall-walk around all four sides of the fourth storey. At that level there is a bedroom over the main stair in the wing, this being reached by a narrow stair over the re-entrant angle. The turret containing the stair may once have had a conical roof later truncated to match the main roof slope. There are gunports in what was originally a dark cellar but which was later divided into a kitchen with a fireplace and two windows and a dairy with one window and a wide western doorway. One gunport commands the doorway in the wing and another opens off the lobby tucked under the base of the staircase. The original hall fireplace is mostly blocked to allow for the new kitchen fireplace flue and there is a smaller new fireplace in the far corner. This room was also then divided into two with a timber partition.

Drumcoltran Tower   *Back view, Drumcoltran Tower*

DRUMMORE NX 136364

Until c1960 remains of a 16th century tower of the Adairs of Kinhilt, occupied by them until at least 1684, stood in a farmyard SW of the village. It measured 11.6m by 6.7m and had a living room 7m long with an ante room at one end over three small vaulted cellars. There was a blocked entrance in the north wall with a spiral stair in an adjacent corner. Direct access to the main room was later provided by an outside stair.

DUNDEUGH NX 602880

Hidden away in trees east of the A713 are remains of late date now too ruined and covered with debris and vegetation to be measurable but which was reported in 1914 to be two buildings, one 10.5m by 6.3m with walls 1m thick, and the other 8m by 5.2m with walls 0.9m thick with a wing 3.7m wide projecting about 2m.

DUNRAGIT NX 150582

The modern mansion of Dunragit house includes part of a 16th century tower with walls 1.5m thick. Two windows with bead and hollow mouldings may be later. Some of the panelling come from Park Castle not far away to the east.

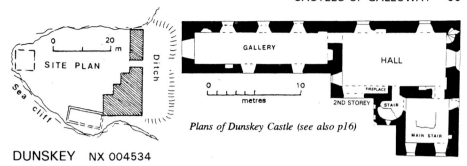

Plans of Dunskey Castle (see also p16)

DUNSKEY NX 004534

The ditch isolating a level promontory with vertical sea cliffs on three sides could be of any period. Footings of a square tower on the point of the promontory may be a remnant of the castle captured and burnt in 1496 by Uchtred McDowell of Garthland and Sir Alexander M'Culloch of Myrton in retaliation for the murder of Dionysius of Hamilton at Wigtown in which deed William Adair of Dunskey was implicated. The existing building occupying the neck of the promontory was built by William Adair, laird from 1546 to 1593 who was married to Helen Kennedy. During this period there occurred the unsavoury episode in which the Abbot of Saulseat Abbey not far to the east was confined and tortured in the castle in an attempt to make him sign away the abbey lands. Dunskey was sold in 1620 to Hew Montgomery and in the 1660s was sold again to John Blair, the Minister of Portpatrick, but it was a ruin by 1684.

The ruin consists of a large L-plan tower house with landward wall of the main block continued to the NW by a two storey block so that the on the inner face of the ditch is an uninterrupted wall 30.4m long by 1.3m thick. The low extension contains the courtyard gateway flanked by a stable and porter's room plus one small cellar below a long gallery with large windows on both sides and at the NW end. This gallery opens off the hall in the main block which has several big windows, a fireplace in a side wall, and a service stair down to one of three cellars below. Two other tiny vaulted cellars are squeezed under the foot of the scale and platt staircase in the wing. A square turret in the re-entrant angle contains the entrance doorway at ground level and the main staircase up from the hall. Being thus positioned there was easy access to the two bedrooms at each of the third and fourth storeys of the main block and three bedrooms in the wing. Little remains of round bartizans on the landward facing corners. It is odd that the well underneath the east end of the landward wall was only made accessible from the ditch, when it could have easily been contained in a projection of some sort. Footings of an outbuilding adjoin the wing.

EARLSTOUN NX 613840

The Berwickshire Sinclairs gained Earlstoun in the mid 16th century and built the tower a few years later. In 1615 it passed to Alexander Gordon of Airds when he married Margaret, heiress of John Sinclair. A stone with the year 1655 and the initials of William Gordon and Mary, second daughter of Sir John Hope of Craigiehall now transferred to the tower was originally fixed to the now almost completely destroyed wing which they added. The scar of its gable came be seen on the east wall. William Gordon was intended to join the church but ended up a soldier fighting under Leslie and Lord Glencairn. After he was killed in a skirmish at Bothwell Bridge the castle was occupied by troops engaged in suppressing Covenanters. The tower is still roofed but serves only as a farm store, having wooden shutters in the windows instead of glass. It measures 10.5m by 6.7m and has two vaulted cellars, a hall above reached by a wide staircase in the wing, and a narrower stair in the re-entrance angle serves three bedrooms including one in the wing at third storey level, plus attic rooms in the roof.

Edingham Castle

*Plans and Section
of Edingham Castle*

EDINGHAM   NX 839626

This early 17th century building measuring 8.6m by 7.2m rose only 5.8m to the eaves and contained just a living room over a vaulted basement divided into two with a wooden partition, plus an attic in the roof. The living room is reached from the entrance by a spiral stair and is now very ruinous, although a blocked fireplace and one window with holes for iron bars still remain in the far end wall.

EGGERNESS   NX 492477

A much altered 16th century tower stands on flat ground overlooking Wigtown Bay.

ENRICK   NX 618545

A ditch defines an oval enclosure 105m by 60m known as The Palace Yard in a flat meadow in which runs a small stream. Foundations of a large oblong building are reported to have been seen near the east end. Edward I is said to have camped here for the winter during one of his campaigns in Scotland.

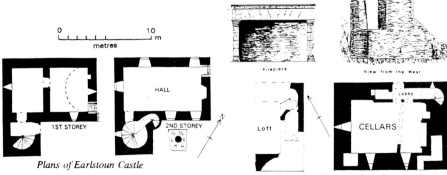

Plans of Earlstoun Castle

Plans and views of Garlies Castle

GALDENOCH NX 974633

This small L-planned ruin at a farm has a panel over the entrance with the year 1547 and the initials of Gilbert, second son of Andrew Agnew of Lochnaw, who lived until 1570. His tower measures 9.1m by 6.4m and contained a vaulted cellar with walls 1.1m thick, a living room, a pair of bedrooms above, and a low and dark attic in the roof, at which level there was also a bedroom over the staircase in the wing. One living room window is set high up to allow a sideboard to be placed beneath it. A narrow second stair allowed direct access from this room to the bedroom furthest from the main staircase. The bartizan closet was reached from that bedroom by a ladder.

GARLIES NX 422692

Alexander III gave the barony of Garlies to Alexander, 4th Hereditary High steward of Scotland in 1263. He was succeeded in 1283 by his second son John who married Margaret, heiress of Sir Alexander Bonkyl of the castle of that name in Berwickshire. From them are descended the Stewarts of Garlies who continued to hold the property until the 20th century and whom became Earls of Galloway in the 1670s. The castle is only accessible by rough tracks from Minnigaff 2.5km to the SW. It consists of the lower part of a late 15th century tower house and a court of some size with numerous outbuildings now too damaged and overgrown to be studied. The site is a shelf slightly above a stream and at the bottom of Glenmalloch Hill. The tower measures 12.5m by 9.3m and has a basement similar to, but a mirror image of, the layout seem at Cardoness and Rusko with a lobby giving access to a tiny guard room, a spiral stair, a narrow wine cellar, and a larger food cellar with one square corner recess. There was the same arrangement of a prison level with the sleeping loft with a hatch into a dungeon pit below. Nothing remains of the upper levels but the hall fireplace has been reset in the wine cellar. Parts of the walls have been patched to preserve them.

HESTAN ISLAND NX 840507

Edward Balliol's seat here is mentioned in documents of the 1340s as a pelum, or palisaded court. Within it would have stood the hall now only 1m high. It was 11m long by 4.5m wide with walls 0.9m thick. There was a doorway in the centre of one long wall and perhaps another off centre in the opposite wall.

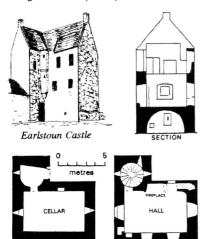

Earlstoun Castle

SECTION

CELLAR

FIREPLACE

HALL

Plans and Section of Galdenoch Castle

Galdenoch Castle

HILLS   NX 912726

Over the tower entrance are the arms and initials of its builder, Edward Maxwell of Breckonside, to whom Hills was granted in 1528, and those of his wife Janet Carson. East of the tower is an inhabited two storey house dated 1721 with square rooms on either side of the entrance and staircase. Reset on it are stones with initials of John Maxwell, Lord Herries, and Edward Maxwell and his wife Agnes. This latter Edward became laird in 1593, built the barmkin gateway soon afterwards and lived until the 1640s. His gateway is decorative rather than defensive, being no more than 3.3m wide by a depth of 1.6m with a total height to the roof ridge of 5.5m. It is similar to another barmkin gateway of c1603 at Harthill Castle in Aberdeenshire. The upper storey slightly projects to contain a porter's room reached by an open stair beside the barmkin wall. On the front are the royal arms. A decorative double row of corbels projects the eaves of the roof still slightly further out. The low wall around the barmkin measuring 20m by 18m is modern except for higher sections either side of the gate.

The tower measures 9m by 7.4m with walls 1.3m thick at basement level rising 13.9m to the top of the parapet. The roof is intact but the only floor surviving above the vault is in a dangerous state. The stair in the NE corner projects into the rooms. Latrines are provided in the SE corner. The hall has recesses on either side of a fireplace in the west wall. A flue backed by a buttress has been created behind the hall fireplace to serve a fireplace inserted into a basement loop, and doorways have been knocked through the east wall into the later house. The third and fourth storeys each contained a single bedroom and there is an attic only reached from the wall-walk. The parapet projects on decorative corbel coursing and has very shallow corner roundels. There are long gargoyles fashioned to resemble cannon barrels draining the wall-walk.

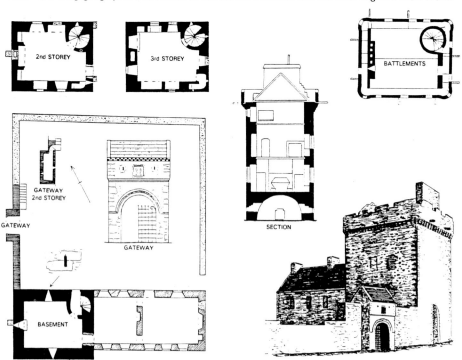

Plans, Section, and Details of Hills Castle

Kenmure Castle

Isle of Whithorn Castle

ISLE OF WHITHORN NX 466366

This still inhabited building lies on a little knoll by the Drumoulin Burn in the middle of the tiny port. It is an L-plan tower with the re-entrant angle almost entirely filled up with a stair projection so that the overall plan is nearly a rectangle with sides of 10.5m by 9m. There are three storeys and an attic, the cellar in the main block being vaults and the third storey having now-inaccessible closets within round bartizans on the west corners. To the east is a single storey range added later and having a probably reset stone with the date 1674 and the initials of Patrick Houston and Margaret Gordon. They may have built the existing stair onto a tower about a century older which once had a staircase in the wing. Several features date from the 19th century when the castle was occupied by Sir John Reid, Superintendent of the Coastguard.

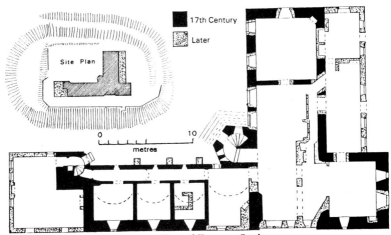

Plans of Kenmure Castle

KENMURE   NX 635764

This castle lies on a large natural mound above the north end of Lock Ken. The early Lords of Galloway fortified the site and it was favoured as a seat by John Balliol. A year after his downfall in 1296 it was acquired by the Gordons of Lochinvar. The castle is said to have been burnt in 1568 after the rout of Queen Mary's army at Langside, and to have been wrecked by Cromwell's troops c1650. It was rebuilt in the 1660s but had again become ruined by the early 19th century when it was restored. It was abandoned after an accidental fire in the 20th century.

The oldest part is a block at the SW corner which preserves two walls of a late 16th century tower house. At fourth storey level there is a round bartizan but otherwise the tower has been mostly remodelled and even its original length is uncertain. There are no signs that it had a vault over the basement. Extending northwards from this part is a long range probably dating from about the time when Sir John Gordon was created Viscount Kenmure by Charles I in the 1630s. There are two upper storeys later subdivided and now filled with trees and collapsing beams over a series of three vaulted cellars and a larger vault, perhaps a kitchen, connected to each other and to a spiral stair in a NE corner turret by a passageway on the east side. The part where this range joined the old tower is that which has suffered the most 19th century remodelling with the insertion of new dividing walls and windows. The east wing and the polygonal staircase tower in the main re-entrant angle are likely to be of the 1660s but the wing has been heavily remodelled. Rope mouldings appear on the windows of this block, which had no vaults, and on the east face of the north wing but it is difficult to tell whether these are original or not, as some evidence is hidden behind harling and the same features appear on an obviously 19th century thinly walled extension of the north wing. Until the 19th century restoration the court was walled in and there was a turret then standing at the NE corner. See plan p103.

Kirkconnel
Tower

KILLASSER   NX 096451

In a field SW of Ardwell church is the base of a tower of c1470-1520 built by the M'Cullochs of Ardwell. It measured 10m by 8.7m over walling mostly 1.9m thick, but the north wall was thicker and half of the east side projected a further 0.7m to contain a stair around the corner.

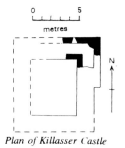

Plan of Killasser Castle

KIRKCONNEL NX 979679

In 1410 Aymer, second son of Sir Herbert de Maxwell of Caerlaverock married the heiress Janet de Kirkconnel. Their descendants built the tower c1550 and have lived in it ever since. The lower part of the exterior is part obscured by later additional buildings and there are a number of alterations, notably the double windows in the south wall lighting the second and third storeys which were inserted by James Maxwell in 1780 on his return to Scotland after exile following the 1745 rebellion. The tower is L-planned with a stair in the wing surmounted by a bedroom at the level of the attic surrounded by a wall-walk and parapet on decorative corbel coursing. The third storey has always been divided into two with a passage to the furthest room from the staircase. The vaulted basement has a pair of cross-shaped loops.

KIRKCUDBRIGHT NX 677508

Malcolm IV is thought to have built an earth and timber castle here after the rebellion of the natives of Galloway in 1160 but the earliest mention of a castle is in 1288 when it was described as having belonged to Alexander III who had died two years earlier. There can be little doubt that he constructed the very fine ashlar faced building of which foundations, now buried again, were discovered by excavation in 1911-13. It may have been left unfinished and would in any case have been destroyed by the Bruces some time after 1308. It was never reoccupied and the charter of James II giving the lands to the burgh does not mention the castle. It is likely, however, that stone from it was used for building Sir Thomas Maclellan's house in the burgh as he had been granted the site in 1577. Only the surrounding ditch now remains visible.

The castle had a wall 2.7m thick around a court 28m long by 17m wide. The NE end was entirely filled with a gatehouse with two round towers 11m in diameter flanking the passageway. The towers had pilaster buttresses above a battered plinth, a feature unique in Scotland and more to be expected c1210 than c1280. One tower lay in the east corner of the court, the other did not quite reach to the north corner which was filled by a round turret containing a spiral staircase. A tower of similar size to those of the gateway but without the pilasters projected from the south corner, whilst straddling the west corner was a tower 13.5m in diameter with a solid basement except for a long passage from the court to a spiral stair in the part facing the field, an unusual arrangement. This tower may have been a keep. See plan on p9.

Killasser Castle

LINCLUDEN   A.M.*   NX 967779

Immediately SE of the ruins of the college is a motte rising 6m in a series of terraces to a summit measuring 7.5m by 4.5m. After the Reformation the eastern range of the college founded by Archibald the Grim, Earl of Douglas shortly before his death in 1400 was doubled in length by Provost Stewart and adapted for use as his private semi-fortified residence. A semi-octagonal turret with gunports was added to contain an entrance and staircase. The series of cellars were each entered independently from the court on the site of the cloister. The north end seems to have been carried up as a high tower and it appears that there was once a hall between it and the staircase.

LOCHFERGUS   NX 699511

This is thought to have been the site of the wooden palace of Fergus, Lord of Galloway in the time of David I. The loch has been drained, leaving the island as an oval platform in a meadow. On it were formerly traces of a building 13.8m long by 5.3m wide with walls 1.2m thick. This was probably a 16th century replacement of a house belonging to the Maclellans of Bombie for the burning of which in 1499 James IV granted remission to Thomas Huchinson and John Cairns.

LOCHINVAR   NX 656853

On an islet measuring just 18m by 15m in the loch are the last traces of a 16th century tower 14.5m long by 10.5m wide with walls 1.5m thick. There are indications of a round staircase turret on the north side. Remains of a bridge to the islet could still be seen in the early 18th century. In 1297 the lands of Lochinvar previously held by the Lord of Galloway were granted to the Gordons who lived here until at least 1640.

LOCH MABERRY   NX 285751

The most southerly of three islands close to the west shore of the loch has a drystone wall 2m thick surviving to a hight of 2m and enclosing an oval court 34m by 25m. On the east side is an enclosure for a boat and within the court are remains of dividing walls and several small buildings, one of which appears to have been built with mortar. It is difficult say what date this belongs to or how long it may have remained in use.

LOCH NAW   NX 994633 & 991628

Among vegetation on a small island near the east shore of the loch is an 8m long and 2.4m thick fragment of a tower house which existed by 1363 when David II made Andrew Agnew keeper of it. In 1390 Archibald the Grim, Earl of Douglas and Lord of Galloway captured and destroyed the castle for some reason now long forgotten. The only features are an aumbry and traces of the basement vault.

In 1426 the Douglases resigned the Bailery of Leswalt back to a later Andrew Agnew. James II made the family hereditary Sheriffs of Galloway (meaning Wigtownshire). By the south end of the loch is tower about 7m square probably built c1550. The inscription "Dom Andreas Agnev 1426 Nomen Domini Fortissima Turris cannot either be original or refer to the present tower, as the lettering is in a style more likely to be 17th century work. The tower has four storeys plus a fifth in the roof within the battlements which are corbelled out. At this level are a caphouse over the staircase, a machicolation over the entrance, and another projection with pistol loops. The tower now stands at one end of an L-shaped three storey mansion replacing the original barmkin. The top storey has attractive dormer windows in the triangular pediments of which are the date 1663 and the initials of Andrew Agnew and his wife Anna Stewart. A wing was added to this building in 1704 and considerable restoration was carried out in the late 19th century. The castle is now used as a restaurant.

LONGCASTLE NX 404473

This castle stood on an artificial island in the former Dowalton Loch the name of which derived from the MacDoualls. Traces of a wall 1.4m thick and of a 10m long building to the south lie hidden away among marsh and scrub some distance from any road.

MACLELLAN'S A.M. NX 683511

In the middle of the town of Kirkcudbright is the well preserved ruin of a large L-planned four storey mansion with a stone over the entrance with the date 1582 and the arms of Sir Thomas Maclellan of Bombie and his wife Dame Grissel Maxwell. The burgh granted the site, which had belonged to the adjacent Franciscan Friary, to Sir Thomas in 1569, and in 1577 added to it the site of the old royal castle, so stone may have been taken from both sites. Sir Thomas was succeeded by his son Robert, who was active in local affairs, and then by his grandson Thomas who fought at the Battle of Philliphaugh in 1645 leading a regiment raised in Galloway at his own expense. His successor, a cousin John, was also involved in the Civil War and these adventures reduced the family fortunes to a point from which they failed to recover. The castle is said to have been roofless since c1752 when it was sold to Sir Robert Maxwell of Orchardton, only to be sold again to the Earl of Selkirk in 1782. It managed to avoid being dismantled for stone and has been in state guardianship since 1912.

The house has a double projection within the re-entrant angle between the long arms of the L and on the outermost angle is a tower containing square private rooms and a wide spiral stair. Two gunports command the entrance and all the windows which could easily be reached from the ground once had iron bars. A straight stair from the entrance rises in a spacious lobby from which there is access to the hall and to a narrow staircase corbelled out of the east wall. Passages run off from the entrance to connect a kitchen with a wide fireplace in the end wall of the wing, and a series of vaulted cellars, including one at the west end which was an ice house for storing meat. On the north side of the main block is a staircase connecting these cellars with the 13.2m long hall with the drawing room beyond to the west. The third storey was similarly divided into a big state room and private room beyond and the top storey in the roof with numerous dormer windows and closets in round corner bartizans was divided into numerous bedrooms. See lower storey plan on page 16.

Lochnaw Castle

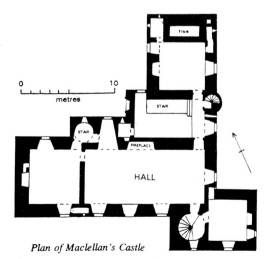

Plan of Maclellan's Castle

Old Print of Maclellan's Castle, Kirkcudbright

MOCHRUM   NX 308541 & 294541

Mochrum was granted by David II to Patrick Dunbar, Earl of March and it was held by his descendants until purchased in 1876 by the Marquis of Bute. In 1474 the barony was divided between the second and third daughters of Patrick Dunbar, the eldest daughter getting his estate of Cumnock. The second daughter and her husband Sir John, son of Alexander Dunbar of Westfield, Sheriff of Moray, then built the tower which became the nucleus of the mansion known as The Old Place of Mochrum, whilst the third daughter and her husband Patrick Dunbar of Kilconquhar provided themselves with a residence on an island in Castle Loch to the west. Their son Patrick left only daughters when he was killed at Flodden in 1513 and by 1590 the island had passed to Sir Patrick Vaus of Barndarroch.

The Old Place of Mochrum was ruined by the late 18th century but was restored by the Marquis of Bute and his successors. It now consists of a courtyard with buildings on all sides. The tower house in the middle of the west side formerly bore the arms of Sir John Dunbar and measures 9m by 7m. There are four storeys, the topmost of which is partly in the roof and has modern dormer windows and access at either end to sections of open parapet on a single row of corbels with corner roundels. Linked to the tower by a modern entrance hall is a T-planned 17th century block 11m long by 5.7m wide with a square staircase turret facing the court. It is more thinly walled than the tower and has four storeys and a central attic with stepped gables.

The remains on the island in Castle Loch are now very ruined and overgrown but were cleared and excavated in 1912 to show evidence of occupation until the 17th century. A wall up to 1m thick enclosed a pear-shaped court 64m by 27m. On the east side was a small harbour with what was probably a boat house adjoining. In the middle of the court is a 13th century chapel which was converted into a hall with service rooms being inserted at the east end, and a solar being added to the west. South of the solar was a kitchen and NE of the hall was a suite of chambers.

The Old Place of Mochrum

MYRTON NX 360432

In 1503 Sir Alexander M'Culloch of Myrton received remission from James IV of a fine imposed for burning Dunskey Castle. Sir Alexander was the King's Master Falconer and in 1504 the estate was made a barony by James IV when he paid a visit while in transit to the Shrine of St Ninian at Whithorn. The tower house was probably built soon afterwards. It stands on what may be a 12th century motte and seems to have had four unvaulted storeys with an attic within a wall-walk with corner roundels. It was ruined by the late 17th century when the surviving southern half was patch up to serve as a dovecote. The mansion north of the tower was built shortly before the M'Cullochs sold Myrton to Sir William Maxwell of Monreith in 1685. He perhaps added the wing to the original main block, now mostly reduced to its lower storey, with a round staircase turret in the middle of the east side. The wing was still occupied in the 19th century, but the Maxwells had by then built Monreith House close to the approach road to which the ruins lie hidden by masses of ivy, shrubs and trees.

OLD RISK NX 448701

Slight traces of a 16th century tower house are said to survive in a remote inaccessible spot 5km NE of Minnigaff.

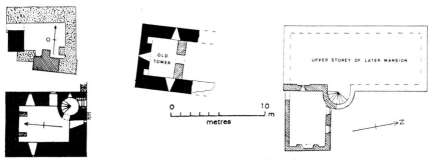

Plans of Mochrum Place   *Plan of Myrton Castle*

Orchardton Tower

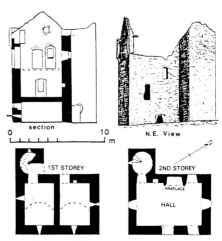

Plans and Section of Plunton Castle

ORCHARDTON   A.M. NX 817551

Orchardton came into the possession of Alexander Carnys, Provost of Lincluden, who died in 1422 and the unusual round tower house was erected by his successor c1450. It stands on a shelf on the side of a low ridge and is accompanied by a tiny court with a range of 16th century cellars on the east side. Above them once lay a hall and in front of it is the base of a stair which once led up to the doorway at the level of the main living room of the tower. South of this stair there appears to have been another wing as there is a latrine shoot here. The tower is 9m in diameter and rises 11m to the top of a parapet carried on a simple plain corbel table. The vaulted basement is a rectangle with the corners cambered off and has a loop on each of three sides and a doorway from the outside in the other. There was no communication with the three round rooms above. The living room has one original window with seats, a fireplace, and a fine ogival headed lavabo or sink. It is reached by a much later stair and doorway on the north side. From this level starts a spiral stair with a latrine at its foot and a caphouse at the top. The bedroom above has two windows with seats and a fireplace and latrine. The top storey was a dark chamber used only by servants.

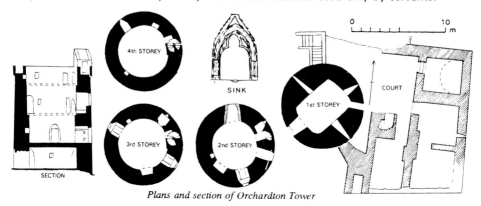

Plans and section of Orchardton Tower

PARK A.M.* NX 189571

Over the entrance of this lofty L-plan building is the inscription "Blessit be the name of the Lord this work vas begvn the first day of March 1590 be Thos Hay and Ionet Mak Dovel his spovs". Thomas was the son of the Thomas Hay who was appointed Abbot of Glenluce Abbey in 1559 but subsequently joined the Reformation party and married a daughter of Kennedy of Bargany. Park Castle remained inhabited over the centuries and until the early 20th century had some low additional buildings around a court to the east. The Scottish Office has now restored the building, recovering it with white harling, the original finish of most towers. The castle lies above the valley in which lie the ruins of Glenluce Abbey. It has a main block measuring 13.3m by 7.6m with walls 1.1m thick. From the entrance at the foot of a wide spiral stair in a square well in the wing a passage runs off to connect two cellars and a kitchen with a wide fireplace in the far end wall. The hall above has its end next the stair screened off to exclude draughts and has on either side of the kitchen fireplace flue a mural chamber and a staircase serving the bedrooms at this end. A top stair in the re-entrant angle serves a garret room over the main stair. See plan on page 16.

PLUNTON NX 605507

Plunton belonged to the M'Ghies in the early 16th century but the tower seems to have been built by the Lennox family to whom the estate passed a generation later. It probably fell into ruin in the 18th century. It stands within a large triangular platform probably of earlier date which appears to have been surrounded by a wet moat. The tower measures 9.1m by 6.4m and is 10m high to the eaves. It contained two vaulted cellars in the basement, a living room above, a pair of bedrooms on the third storey and a low attic for servants in the roof. The cellar furthest from the staircase wing has a gunport commanding the approach and has its own doorway to the outside with communication with the rest of the tower. At the summit there were closets contained in small round corner bartizans. The two surviving ones have tiny shotholes and there is another at the top of wing commanding the entrance.

Plunton Castle

Park Castle

PORT NX 426358

Nothing is known of the history of this remote cliff-top site 0.5km east of St Ninian's Cave and 1km south of Physgill House. It consists of a court roughly 19m square with the two landward sides enclosed by 2m high walls 1.7m thick meeting at a rounded northern angle. There are traces of buildings close to the cliff edge but inspection is difficult because of the gorse covering and obscuring the site.

RAVENSTONE NX 410443

The Maclellans built a tower c1560 on lands formerly held by the M'Dowalls. In the mid 17th century it passed to Robert Stewart, a younger son of the 2nd Earl of Galloway and the tower was widened into a double gabled house. It was then known as Castle Stewart. Later wings have been removed and the original part restored.

RUSKO NX 584605

This tower, rather oddly sited at the foot of a slope descending from the B796 road, was built by Robert Gordon sometime after his marriage to the heiress of Sir Robert Corsane (or Ackerson), and before the latter's death in 1520. Robert Gordon assumed the title Glenskyreburn, the former name of this estate, but succeeded to the lordship of Lochinvar on his brother's death at the Battle of Flodden in 1513. Sir John Gordon of Lochinvar is recorded as living at Rusko in 1574. The tower has remained habitable and was thoroughly restored in the late 1970s. The tower measures 11.9m by 9.1m and is entered through a doorway with a joggled flat arch with round corners. The shields in a panel above are now defaced but one is said to have once had the figure 65, presumably for the year 1565, although the tower is certainly at least half a century older than that. The arrangements are copied from those of Cardoness and Garlies with the doorway opening onto a lobby off which open the spiral stair, a porter's room, and a doorway to the cellar over which is a sleeping loft. The cellar has one round recess for grain storage and may once have been divided in two with a second doorway from the lobby. Above the vault are the hall, a suite of two rooms on the fourth storey, and an attic in the roof. There is a plain parapet carried on a double row of corbels the lower row of which is purely decorative and carries nothing. The stair is crowned by a gabled caphouse. The base has been cleared out of a two storey wing of 1600 to the north which was a ruin by the late 18th century. It has in the middle of the south wall a projecting square staircase turret.

SHIRMERS NX 657743

In the steading of Shirmers Farm is an overgrown fragment about 2m high of one end wall of a 16th century tower 6.3m wide built by the Gordons. There were no vaults and the hall floor was carried on an internal offset. The tower is said to have been burnt after Queen Mary's defeat at Langside in 1568.

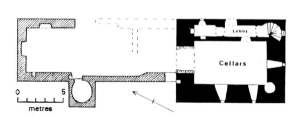

Plan of Rusko Castle

Plan of Port Castle

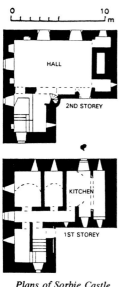

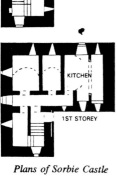

Plans of Sorbie Castle

Rusco Castle

SINNINESS NX 205531

Just one fragment of an end wall remains of a building 14m by 8.2m mostly only represented by buried footings. It was built against a bank so that only two sides of the basement were freestanding. It is said to have been built by Archibald Kennedy c1600 and to have passed to the Dalrymple Earl of Stair. It was still in use in 1684 but probably was abandoned soon afterwards as Lord Stair had numerous other seats.

SORBIE NX 451471

Generally known as The Old Place of Sorbie, this castle was built by Alexander Hannay, who took over the estate in 1569 and lived until at least 1612. It is similar to Park Castle in general arrangements and was probably begun c1600. Protection was certainly needed from unruly neighbours as the Hannays were at feud with the Murrays of Broughton and there were a series of disturbances also involving the Stewarts of Garlies and the Kennedys and Dunbars. The Hannays became impoverished and in 1626 much of the estate was sold to Sir Patrick Agnew of Lochnaw and Stewart of Garlies, while in 1640 John Hannay was killed in a quarrel. Stewart of Garlies, by then Earl of Galloway, became laird of Sorbie in 1677. The last resident in the castle was Brigadier-General John Stewart, M.P. for Wigtown in 1707 and lived until 1748. The remains were in a much ruined and overgrown state until tidied up and made safe for visitors by members of the Hannay clan. A cobbled courtyard and footings of a rectangular outbuilding were exposed.

Sorbie Castle

The main block measures 12.5m by 7.2m and has a kitchen and two cellars connected by a passage to the entrance and scale-and-platt staircase in the wing. This stair only rises to hall level from which a spiral stair is corbelled out in the re-entrant angle. All the upper rooms could be reached directly from this stair so there is no secondary staircase as at Park, the kitchen fireplace flue having small chambers on either side at the upper levels. The wing also contained bedrooms, giving seven of them in all in addition to the attic in the main block roof. The fourth storey rooms had closets in now-destroyed round bartizans. As at Park there was a lobby screened off at the stair end of the hall, here having the extra luxury of its own fireplace.

STRANRAER   A.M.   NX 061608

This tower was built in the first half of the 16th century by the Adairs of Kinhilt and later belonged to the Kennedys and then the Dalrymples of Stair. It originally has four storeys plus an attic within an open wall-walk, but in the late 17th century the tower was adapted for use as the town gaol and headquarters of Graham of Claverhouse whilst he was Sheriff of Wigtown and campaigning against the Covenanters. A new top storey retaining the original parapet then replaced the attic and wall-walk on the main block whilst the wing was given a sloping roof with crenellated gables and an open bell turret. Until the 1970s the tower was neglected and hidden by later adjacent buildings which have now been cleared away. It measures 10.6m by 8.6m with walls 1.7m thick except on the north side where they contained a passage connecting the entrance, two cellars, and a spiral stair in a shallow wing. The cellar vaults are of differing axes, perhaps as a result of alterations which have included altering the entrance lobby and driving a passageway through the wing below the stair outer part.

THREAVE   A.M.*   NX 739623

This castle lies on the west side of a flat 20 acre island in the River Dee 2.5km west of Castle Douglas. The island would have formed ample pasturage for the cattle of the garrison in times of trouble. There was probably a timber house and outbuildings on the island in the 13th century as the island burnt by Edward Bruce in 1308 is assumed to have been Threave. The large tower house was begun by Archibald The Grim shortly after he was created Lord of Galloway by David II in 1369. He later became 3rd Earl of Douglas and died at Threave in 1400, being succeeded by his son Archibald, who was granted the title of Duke of Touraine in France. After he was killed at the Battle of Verneuil in 1424 his widow Margaret, sister of James I, ruled Galloway for a quarter of a century from her seat at Threave. During the minority of James II the young 6th Earl of Douglas and his brother were murdered in Edinburgh Castle in 1440 at the so called "Black Dinner" instigated by the regents Livingstone and Crichton. In 1452 James II invited the 8th Earl to dinner at Stirling to settle differences and in a burst of anger stabbed him to death. James, the 9th Earl not surprisingly harboured a grudge and plotted with the English. About this time a hall block and another range near the tower pulled down to provide space and materials for the hurried construction of a loopholed wall with three round flanking towers around the tower house. In 1455 James II marched against the Douglases and besieged Threave Castle with his artillery. The garrison surrendered eventually but subsequent payments to the officers suggest bribery proved more effective than the cannon James II was so proud of and which were to cost him his life in an explosion at the siege of Roxburgh Castle in 1460.

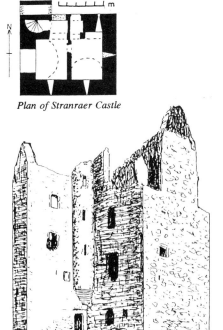

Plan of Stranraer Castle

Stranraer Castle

The Old Place of Sorbie

The castle remained a royal fortress for the remainder of its life. It was then more of a fort than a residence apparently lacking permanent accommodation other than that in the tower house. Its keepers, generally also Stewards of Kirkcudbright, had their principal seats elsewhere. Under James III Threave was held by his consort Margaret of Denmark until 1474 when Robert, grandson of Lord Carlyle of Torthorwald had custody. Subsequent keepers were the Earl of Angus, the Earl of Bothwell, and Sir John Dunbar of Mochrum. After he was killed at Flodden in 1513 the castle and Stewardship went to Robert Maxwell and in 1525 were declared to be hereditary in his family. After being captured by the English at Solway Moss in 1542 Lord Maxwell was obliged to support his captors and in 1545 Threave Castle was captured by the forces of the Regent Arran. The castle was also briefly lost again in 1588 after James VI accused the Maxwells of complicity in Catholic plots. Robert Maxwell, newly created Earl of Nithsdale, garrisoned Threave with 70 men for the King in 1638, later increasing this force to 100 men. In 1640 the castle was besieged for 13 weeks by a force of Covenanters, being surrendered on very honourable terms in September in the orders of the King. The explicit instructions to the laird of Balmaghie for the destruction of the vault and battlements were luckily not carried out, and whatever timberwork was removed was reinstated during the Napoleonic Wars when the tower was used to accommodate prisoners. It fell into ruin again and was handed over for preservation by the state in 1913. A ferry service is provided for visitors.

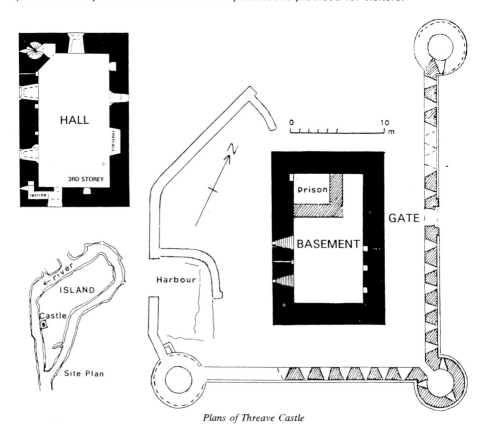

Plans of Threave Castle

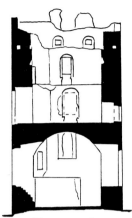

Threave: section

*Threave
Castle*

The tower house is 18.4m long by 12.1m wide with walls 2.1m thick above the vault supporting the hall floor and 2.4m thick below it. They rose about 21m to the top of the parapet. There were two storeys below the vault and three above, and probably an attic within the wall-walk. There are entrances into hall and the kitchen below. The dark cellar was reached only by a hatch in the kitchen floor and another hatch gave access to a square prison divided off in the NW corner. The kitchen has a large fireplace and latrine and presumably also functioned as a mess-hall for servants. A spiral stair in the NW corner leads up from it to the wall-walk. The hall also has a big fireplace and was lighted by three windows with mullions and transoms in embrasures with seats. It has a latrine above that of the kitchen in the SW corner. The storey above had two rooms with fireplaces forming a suite for the lord. His living room was next the stair and his bedroom was beyond, with a latrine above the others. The fifth storey formed a single large room with numerous windows but neither latrine or fireplace and was presumably a dormitory for servants and retainers. the roof was carried on great beams starting below and going through this storey. The triple row of holes are thought to have been nesting boxes for pigeons. The shaft running round in the wall was probably intended to contain bonding timbers to help carry the roof.

Around the tower and only 4.4m away from it on the south and east sides is the much more ruined wall of the mid 15th century. It is 1.4m thick above a battered plinth rising out of the water filled ditch and is pierced by loops 2m apart. The three most vulnerable corners had round towers up to 5.5m in diameter but only that to the SE now stands above the base, although there is a large fallen chunk of that to the SW. The surviving tower has a basement with three gunloops, an upper storey level with the main wall-walk, and a battlemented stage above. The courtyard was entered through a gateway closed by a drawbridge with a yett or wooden door behind it. On the west side the court is 12m wide and contains a harbour for small boats which along with the 1.1m thick base of the river wall was only uncovered in the late 1970s. On the north there is a section of the court facing the river which there was insufficient time to wall in before the siege. It was closed by an earth bank.

Wreath's Tower

Kenmure Castle

URR   NX 815647

This impressive but overgrown earthwork castle is remarkable for having a large and well preserved bailey, a rarity in Scotland and possibly an older earthwork modified by one of the 12th century Lords of Galloway. The bailey is an oval 140m long by 75m wide and entirely surrounds the motte which rises 11m above a deep surrounding ditch to a summit 30m across. See the plan on page 6.

WIGTOWN   NX 437550

The castle lay below the hill on which stands the town, a position allowing defence by marshland and wet moats and the possibility of direct access for sea-going vessels. The castle was probably built by Alexander III in the 1260s and was demolished by the Bruces after occupation by the English. In 1342 David II created Sir Malcolm Flemming Earl of Wigtown and keeper of the castle but it does not appear that it was in fact ever restored. Foundations could be seen in 1830 but nothing is now visible of either walls or moats, nor has anything survived of the embattled tower William Hannay was licensed in 1549 to build "on the north side of the Hie Gaitt" of the burgh of Wigtown.

WREATH'S   NX 953565

Only a fragment 8m high of the corner containing the spiral stair remains of an early 16th century tower held by Regent Morton at the time of his execution in 1581, after which it went to the Maxwells. The walls were 1.7m thick at the level of the vaulted basement, and there is evidence of two of at least three assumed upper storeys.

LIST OF EARTHWORKS

ARDWELL NX 107455 7m high mound, 21m across on top, 450m E of A. House

ANWOTH NX 575551 Two platforms divided by ditch 0.5km SW Cardoness Castle. Total length of 110m. 25m wide at SE end where it is 7m high.

BALGREGGAN NX 097506 mound 7.5m high with summit 18m by 16m, on ridge commanding coastal views north of Sandhead Village.

BALMACLELLAN NX 653793 Summit 12m across, 4m high above ditch. On ridge north of village. There is space by the mound for a possible bailey.

BARBROCKWOOD NX 459654 Mound 4m high with narrow 19m long summit above Palnure Burn 4.5km east of Newton Stewart.

BARMAGACHAN NX 613493 Mound by farm lane 2km NE of Borgue Church. 6m high with summit 18m by 16m Ditch to SW.

BORELAND NX 647517 Big mound 6m high to summit 35m by 26m 3km SW of Twynholm. Surrounding ditch with outer bank 4m high on north.

BORELAND NX 355586 Overgrown mound 6m high By B733 opposite B. Farm.

CALLY NX 606556 Mound in trees 4m high, 24m across on top, east of Cally Loch.

CAMBELTOWN NX 659539 Terrace sided mound near Twynholm. Top 25m by 15m.

COLVEND NX 869542 Small overgrown mound bearing ruined cottage by track.

CRAILLOCH NX 327526 Crag east of C. Farm cut through to make small mound.

CULDOACH NX 706537 Damaged motte now 2.5m high, 26m by 14m on top, between farmhouse and the ravine of a small stream.

DALRY NX 619813 Overgrown mound 34m by 31m on top 4.5m high on east, higher above Water of Ken to west. North of Dalry parish church.

DINNANCE NX 676638 Rock motte 1km SW of Laurieton 15m by 8.5m on top.

DROUGHDOOL NX 148568 Overgrown mound 8m high, 12m across on top in clearing of woods by A715 near school.

DRUCHTAG NX 347432 9m high mound, 20m across on top, near Mochrum village.

DRUMMORE NX 130359 High spur between two streams SW of castle site cut by ditch to make motte with 12m diameter dished top. 3m above land to west.

EDGARTON NX 674631 Ridge east of farm cut off by ditch at each end, that on south having a counterscarp bank. Summit measures 25m by 13m. Steep drop to west.

ERNESPIE NX 782629 Mound 3.5m high in woods by stream 2km NE Castle Douglas. Summit measures 25m by 15m at the SW and 9.5m at the NE.

GLASSERTON NX 404371 Ditch 9m wide & 1.5m deep isolates spur SSW G. House.

INGLESTON NX 982651 Motte 3.5m high, 26m by 17m on top, behind farm.

INGLESTON NX 775579 Natural knoll NE of farm and 0.7km SE of Gelston scarped into motte 5m high and 21m by 13m on top.

INNERMESSAN NX 084633 Motte 27m across 5m high above ditch on north set on a high spur between sea and ravine of Kirclachie Burn.

KIRKCARSWELL NX 754487 Mound with 13m square summit 3.5m high above ditch to east and higher on west with stream to north. 1km NE Dundrennan Church.

KIRKCLAUGH NX 534521 Above 30m high sea-cliff below coast road 1km SE of Barholm. Overgrown mound in trees 18m across and 6m high above ditch separating it from a boomerang shaped bailey to the west and north.

KIRKCORMACK NX 716574 By disused graveyard east of River Dee 4km NE of Tongland Church is overgrown mound 4m high above ditch. Summit 18m by 20m.

LINDOWIE NX 154674 Drystone causeway links small promontory with mainland on a spur where Lindowie Burn meets Water of Luce, 3.5km NE of New Luce.

LOCHRINNE NX 722871 14m wide platform tapering to nothing. Divided by ditch into two parts 33m and 25m long. Beyond stream from A702 6km Sw Moniave.

MACHARS HILL (The Beacon) NX 470653 4m high mound by stream on lower spur of Cairnsmore of Fleet 6km north of Creetown. Summit 14m by 9m.

MINNIGAFF NX 410665 Wide and deep ditch through promontory above River Cree and Penkill Burn protects platform 13m wide tapering to a point 32m away.

PARLIAMENT KNOWE NX 427662 Mound 3m high, 29m diameter on top west of A712, 2km east of Newton Stewart.

PARTON NX 694709 Mound 27m by 14m on top rising 12m above stream. Natural ramp breaks line of surrounding ditch.

PARTON NX 697698 Fine mound 8m high from surrounding ditch to summit 15m across beside Loch Ken near Parton Church.

PULCREE NX 593583 Mound 3m high and 18m square on top in trees on ridge near quarry by west bank of Water of Fleet between Rusko and Gatehouse of Fleet.

ROBERTON NX 604486 Rectangular mound 6m high and 27m by 13.5m on top by Putwhirren Burn about 2.5km west of Borgue Church.

SKAITH NX 381662 Homestead moat in trees by lane SE of Skaith Farm.

SORBIE NX 451469 Terraced mound 3m high, 16m square on top, near castle.

SOUTHWICK NX 937570 2m high round platform 23m across by stream 1km Se of Caulkerbush Church, opposite Home Farm on A710 coast Road.

TROQUEER NX 975748 Mound 10m above meadows of Nith and 5.5m high to north with summit 39m by 38m. Damaged slightly by Dumfries suburbia to north.

TROSTRIE NX 656574 Large rectangular mound behind farm from 7m to 12m high.

TWYNHOLM NX 664543 Mound 5.5m high, 14m by 11m on top. Site now built over.

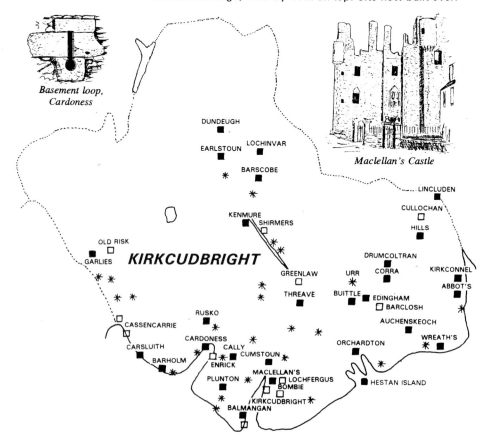

Basement loop, Cardoness

Maclellan's Castle

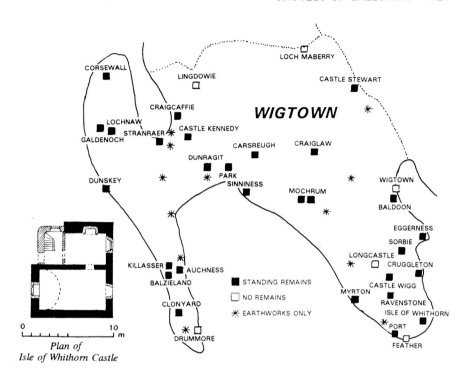

Plan of
Isle of Whithorn Castle

Cassencarrie Castle

GAZETTEER OF CASTLES IN LANARK AND RENFREW

BARCRAIG NS 397565

At the south end of Barcraigs Reservoir the B776 road cuts into the featureless last fragment 1.4m thick and 3m high of a small late 16th century tower house.

BAROCHAN NS 415686

A much altered 16th century tower of the Fleming family forms the nucleus of a 19th century mansion 2km NNE of the village of Houston.

BARR NS 347582

In parkland overlooking Barr Loch is a ruined tower of c1520 measuring 10.8m by 7.9m. There are traces of a small court to the west and south with the entrance and gunport on the north side. Late 19th century drawings show more of the court and the outbuilding it had on the west side, and also the lost parapet carried on four continuously corbelled courses and north gable of the tower. A roof mark shows that there was once a two storey outbuilding south of the tower. From the late 16th century until the late 18th century Barr was owned by the Ferguslie Hamiltons. A lintel at the foot of stair has the date 1680 and the initials L.H.I.C, and the unusually high parapet with round bartizans once bore the year 1699 with the initials W.O. Of about the same period is the present pedimented entrance doorway with the initials I.W.M.H.

The new entrance leads onto a passage connecting a cellar at the south end and a kitchen to the north with the spiral stair in the NW corner. The original entrance was in the north wall beside the kitchen fireplace flue, beyond which is a mural chamber. The hall has a fireplace in the west wall, two big lockers, and three windows of the embrasure of one of which is reached a second smaller stair in the SW corner allowing direct access to the rooms at this end on the subdivided third and fourth storeys.

Barr Castle

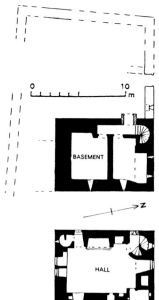

Plans of Barr Castle

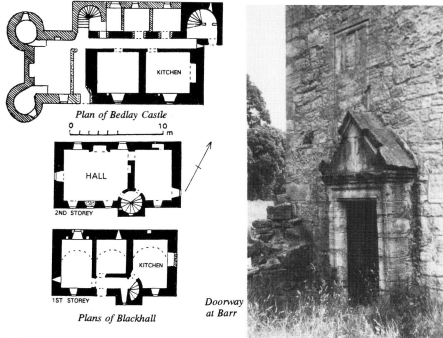

Plan of Bedlay Castle

0   10
                       m

HALL

2ND STOREY

KITCHEN

1ST STOREY

Plans of Blackhall

Doorway
at Barr

BEDLAY   NS 692700

Robert, 4th Lord Boyd of Kilmarnock built a castle on the end of a volcanic crag after obtaining the estate from his kinsman James, Archbishop of Glasgow in 1580. James, 8th Lord Boyd disposed of Bedlay in 1642 to the Advocate James Roberton of Earnock, whose descendants held it until 1786. James Campbell of Petershill purchased the castle in c1805. The main block measures 13m by 7.4m and had a square stair turret at the NE corner flanking both the north and east walls. The doorway is unusually placed in the lesser re-entrant angle because the approach is from that side. A passage from it leads to a kitchen and cellar and now leads onto the lowest level of a late 17th century extension with round turrets on the west corners. As the ground falls away on this side the towers have lower basement rooms reached by stairs covered by trapdoors in the floor of the room thought to have been intended as a second kitchen. A square stair turret was added where the old and new parts meet on the north side with a single storey range of offices between it and the original stair wing. There is access from a removable window seat in the SW tower to a low hidden room below. The terrace south of the castle is probably of the same period as the main block as its supporting wall is old, but the balustrade is somewhat later.

BLACKHALL   NS 490630

This house of c1600, built by a Stewart descended from John of Ardgowan, an illegitimate son of Robert III, was restored from ruin in the 1980s. A stair in a shallow projection has a shot-hole commanding the entrance and connects the two vaulted cellars and kitchen in the basement with the hall and private room above and the three bedrooms with dormer windows in the roof. The building measures 14m by 6.7m and has walls up to 1m thick. The private room has a latrine in the north wall. See p19.

BOGHALL   NS 041370

The Fleming family obtained Biggar by marriage in the late 13th century. In 1458 James II gave this branch a peerage with the title Lord Fleming of Cumbernauld, and in 1605 James VI revived the Earldom of Wigtown, originally granted by Robert Bruce to the Galloway branch of the family, to the then Lord Fleming. The 6th and last Earl died in 1747. The castle forming their chief seat took its name from its flat marshy site south of Biggar. It is said to have been founded in the 15th century although the surviving fragments and old drawings suggest a mainly mid 16th century building. A low fragment of a stair turret survives of the main three storey domestic block on the south side of a pentagonal court about 60m across. The turret stood complete but badly cracked a century ago but fell soon afterwards and a plaque records repairs to the stump in 1912. The gatehouse on the north side of the court has vanished and so has the round corner tower standing near the domestic block but fragments exist of two other D-shaped towers with gunports at each of two storeys which were vaulted and made semi-octagonal. The better preserved northern tower is about 4.5m in external diameter and has an offset below the upper level of gunports and continuous corbelling for an open wall-walk. On it is a shield with the Fleming arms and the year 1670 reset from the fallen upper stage of the stair turret.

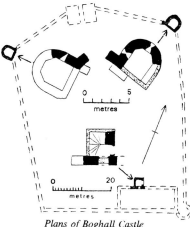

Plans of Boghall Castle

North Tower, Boghall Castle

Stair Turret, Boghall Castle

BOTHWELL A.M.* NS 688594

Bothwell was originally held by the Olifards and in 1242 passed to Walter de Moravia (Murray) who dated a charter here in 1278 and is assumed to have then had the present castle on a low sandstone crag above a delightful sweep of the Clyde under construction. The castle was designed as a pentagonal court extending 70m from a the south wall on the cliff edge to a gateway with twin flanking round towers over 10m in diameter. Other towers of similar size were planned at the two eastern corners while the short SW side had at one end a small round tower flanking a postern and a huge four storey round tower keep 20m in diameter. In the event this SW part of the castle which is faced with very fine sandstone ashlar was the only part to be built either before funds ran out or the death of Alexander III precipitated the Scots' struggle for independence. Footings survive of the gatehouse and NE tower and of two square latrine turrets, and there is a wide dry ditch beyond them, but the curtain walls themselves were clearly never even begun. Thus the castle which was stormed by the Scots in 1299 after a fourteen month blockade of Stephen de Brampton and his garrison must have had its bailey mostly defended by wooden palisades. See p8-9.

In September 1301 Edward I of England recaptured Bothwell Castle after a siege of a month in which a wooden belfry constructed at Glasgow was with some difficulty and expense brought here and placed against the defences for an assault. The keep then became the headquarters of Aymer de Valance, Earl of Pembroke in his role as Warden of Scotland, and he was granted the barony of Bothwell by King Edward in 1301. In 1311 there was a garrison of 28 squares and 29 archers at Bothwell under the command of Sir Walter Fitzgilbert. After the English defeat at Bannockburn in 1313 Sir Walter surrendered the castle and various fugitives within it including the Earl of Hereford to Edward Bruce who slighted the defences. In 1336 Edward III stayed a month at Bothwell during his campaign in support of Edward Balliol. He had the wooden defences patched up and the master-mason John de Kilburne began work on building a new stone hall of which only a few courses and a fireplace survive. In March 1337 the castle was taken for a second time by means of a belfry when the rightful owner Sir Andrew de Moray, Warden of Scotland, besieged it. He is said to have destroyed it to the foundations and although this was clearly an exaggeration this must refer to when the western half of the mighty keep was tumbled into the Clyde.

Bothwell Castle

Interior of keep, Bothwell

SE Tower, Bothwell

Bothwell Castle was only restored after 1362 when David II granted the barony to Archibald the Grim, later Lord of Galloway and still later third Earl of Douglas. In later years Bothwell was his chief seat and the present east and north walls of what had become a reduced court just 27m wide are attributed to him. Buttresses at either end of the north front have remains of large round bartizans similar to those appearing on other Scottish castles of c1375-1400. The south wall, which has a square latrine turret and is pierced by large windows of a chapel and former apartments, plus the two storey hall block and the noble four storey SE tower with the base of a machicolated parapet are thought to be the work of the 4th Earl, who was killed on military service for the King of France in 1424. Also of that period was the tower about 12m square at the NE corner of the reduced court which seems to have been built on late 13th or early 14th century foundations and is now mostly destroyed. It served as the principal tower during this period, containing the lord's private rooms, and has on its west face the grooves of a drawbridge by which it was entered before the hall was built against it. Slezer's drawing of 1693 shows a gateway tower presumably of this period of which nothing has survived standing where the present entrance is. After the Black Douglases were defeated and forfeited by James II in 1455 Bothwell was granted to Lord Crichton, whose son William was in turn forfeited in 1484, and then to Sir John Ramsey who was also forfeited in 1488. Bothwell was granted to Lord Hailes but in 1492 was exchanged for Hermitage and thus passed to Archibald Douglas, 5th Earl of Angus. James IV visited the castle in 1503 and 1504. It was probably just prior to this that the hall was remodelled, vaults being inserted in the basement and the row of ten clerestory windows being added on the west side.

In 1584 Dame Margaret Maxwell, Countess of Angus was ordered by the Privy Council to surrender the castle, in which she lived, because of suspected complicity with her nephew, Lord Maxwell, then in rebellion. She was back there by 1594 when it was noted at court that masses were being celebrated in the castle, the Maxwells still being catholics. In 1669 Archibald Douglas, 1st Earl of Forfar acquired Bothwell and in the 1690s demolished the NE tower and gatehouse and the inner walls of the southern apartments to provide materials for a new mansion immediately to the east which was demolished in 1926. His son was killed at Sherrifmuir in 1715 and after a celebrated law-suit Bothwell and other Douglas estates went to Archibald Stewart of Grandtully and his wife Jane, sister of the 1st Duke of Douglas. It now belongs to their descendant the Earl of Home but has been in state guardianship since 1935.

The keep rises 27m from the bottom of a dry moat dividing it from the court. A drawbridge pit is in turn divided off from the moat and has a postern which could only have been reached by a ladder. The keep has an angular projection to contain the entrance which was closed by a portcullis and led via a rib vaulted dog-leg passage to a hall formerly covered by a wooden vault carried on a central pier rising through the basement below. The hall and the two storeys above each have passages to latrines in the SW curtain wall. The hall has a single light window with seat in the embrasure facing the court. The room above is thought to have been a mess hall for retainers and now only has windows in the comparatively thin straight wall built c1370 to make the tower habitable again after the 1337 destruction. At that level there is a guard room over the entrance and access via the spiral staircase onto the top of the curtain to the north. The doorway here was barred against the keep rather than the curtain. From the laird's private room with a fine two light window overlooking the court there was access onto the wall-walk of the SW curtain.

BUSBY NS 594561

The small four storey 16th century tower with chequered corbelling for the parapet known as The Peel lies above Kittock Water. It was owned in 1607 by James Hamilton and in 1793 was held by Andrew Houston of Jordanhill. It now forms the NW corner of a house of the 18th century and later and has been somewhat altered.

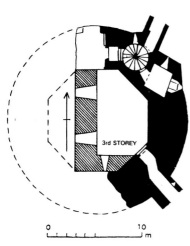

Plan of the keep at Bothwell

Busbie Peel

CADZOW   NS 734537

Cadzow was an important Hamilton seat and now lies in the park of the mansion of Chatelherault named after a French Dukedom granted to the family in the 1540s.The castle lies directly above the wooded ravine of the Clyde but is overlooked by higher ground to the west on the other side of a dry ditch and a track running down to an adjacent bridge. The remains are very ruined and overgrown and not easily understood but the layout and development seem to have had some similarities with the Hamiltons' other castle at Craignethan. Probably there was some sort of principal dwelling in the middle of a small court built up on still-surviving vaulted cellars built against a core of native rock. The less well defended rectangular outer court on the north side was probably added later. One of the exposed corners of the inner court has the base of a round flanking tower no doubt once containing gunports. For further details of the history of Cadzow and the Hamiltons see under Craignethan.

CALDERWOOD   NS 658560

A modern house high above the Calder Burn near Crossbasket stands on the site of a big early Maxwell tower 12m wide by 21m long by 26m high which fell down in 1773. The house incorporates outbuildings of little interest built against the tower.

CALDWELL   NS 422551

On moorland above Lugton Water west of Neilston is a 16th century tower of the Mures with renewed battlements upon chequered corbelling. The vaulted basement has its own doorway in the west wall. An outside stair serves an upper doorway on the north side. There are shot-holes in the breasts of the upper windows.

CASTLEMILK   NS 608594

This is a massive late 15th century Stewart tower of three storeys plus a modernised attic with a wall-walk with a plain parapet. There are new windows and a big round arched west doorway plus substantial later additions. The original doorway was beside the staircase in the SE corner which now lacks its original caphouse. There are chambers, said to be hiding places, on either side of the hall fireplace.

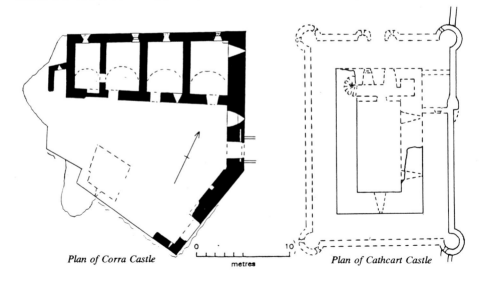

Plan of Corra Castle   *Plan of Cathcart Castle*

0   10
metres

CATHCART   NS 586599

Glasgow City Council had this ruin high above the River Cart destroyed to its foundations in 1980 on the pretext that it was dangerous. There was a subsequent outcry, and the remains have since been tidied up and excavated. Cathcart belonged to a family of that name from the 12th century until it passed to Lord Sempill in 1546. In the early 19th century one of the Cathcarts repurchased the estate and was created Earl of Cathcart. The castle was already ruined by then, having been abandoned in favour of a new house c1740. It was partly dismantled for materials until this was realised to be unremunerative. The building comprised a four storey tower 15.5m by 9.2m of about the time of the peerage granted to the Cathcarts in 1447. The thin curtain wall surrounding it at a distance of 3m and having round corner turrets and a twin-turreted gateway was probably added slightly later. There seems to have been a second court also with round turrets to the east towards the approach. The tower east wall was thickened to contain mural chambers and the entrance and stairs. The hall had two small closets in the walls, five windows, and a fireplace on the south side. The storey above seems to have been subdivided, perhaps as a later alteration.

CORRA   NS 972482

On a promontory above cliffs to the Corra Linn falls on the Clyde are remains of the the Bannatynes' castle of Corra or Corehouse. They originally held the estate from Kelso Abbey and lived here until Sir James Bannatyne sold up to William Somerville of Cambusnethan in 1695. A bridge over a ditch leads to a segmental arched entrance in a wall 1.4m thick on the landward side of a pentagonal court 22m across. A vaulted cellar, and an oven and drain probably of a kitchen, remain of a block overlooking the Clyde. On the other side, overlooking a tributary valley, is a better preserved block with a private room at the east end of a hall with four vaulted cellars below. Three of the cellars have their own doorways directly from the court. Above the private room was a bedroom. It does not appear that there were any rooms over the hall.

Corra Castle

Covington Tower

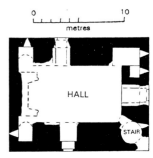

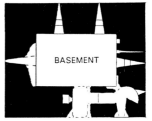

Plans of Covington Tower

COUTHALLY   NS 972482

Couthally was the chief seat of the Somervilles before they moved to Drum in Midlothian. The last remnants of the castle lie on a flat moorland and were perhaps protected by wet moats. There are fragments of a tower 22m long by 10.5m wide although it may have only attained this size as a result of 16th century alterations, a wing being added on the south and a round tower on the other side facing two courts.

COVINGTON   NS 975399

The shallow ditch to the west and south may be a relic of a moated timber house of the Keiths who whom Covington was granted by Robert Bruce. It passed to the Lindsays who built the massive tower in the mid 15th century, and in the 17th century was sold to Sir George Lockhart, President of the Court of Session. only a round dovecot near the road remains of various later outbuildings. The tower measures 15.3m by 12m and has four storeys with the hall on the third storey above the former vault of a sleeping loft. There are remains of mural chambers on either side of where the fireplace was in the east wall and a third chamber in the SW corner. The NW corner contains a spiral stair all the way up to the roof from the entrance into the basement in the north wall. The basement west wall contains a sink and drain.

CRAIGNEITH   NS 663553

The large ruin high above the east bank of the Calder has an old tower as its nucleus.

CRAIGNETHAN   A.M.*   NS 816464

In c1531 Sir James Hamilton of Finnart, a bastard son of James, 1st Earl of Arran, and guardian of the infant 2nd Earl, began construction of a castle of very advanced design on a spur formed by the ravines of the Water of Nethan and Craignethan Burn. It has a rectangular court 49m long by 25m wide with three storey towers measuring about 11m by 10m at the east corners, a tower containing a right angled gateway passage on the north side, a staircase turret on the south side and west front as much as 5m thick with a ditch in front containing a caponier (a vaulted chamber with gunloops) reached from the staircase in the SW corner tower. This side was vulnerable to cannon fire as it faced higher ground and the innovative caponier provided flanking fire in a way invisible to and invulnerable to attackers. Heavy cannon could be mounted on top of the west wall, and there are ports for handguns elsewhere, those in the east towers being placed high up to command the slopes of the ravines which were then bare but are now covered in trees. A second entrance on the south side was abandoned whilst the castle was being built. Between the east towers is a range of cellars below courtyard level. An intended range above them was never built.

Occupying most of the eastern part of the court is a tower house 21.2m long by 16m wide. It was kept low so that the west curtain could protect it from cannonfire, the west side containing the entrance being about 11.3m high to the former top of a parapet supported on a decorative double row of corbelling and having roundels at the corners. There is an extra roundel and also a worn armorial panel over the entrance A fall in ground level allows the other walls to descend further around a series of vaulted storage cellars. The building is divided lengthways by a spine wall above which was the central gully of the former double gabled roof. South of this wall is the lofty barrel vaulted great hall with three large windows, a musicians gallery reached from the staircase off the entrance lobby, and a fireplace in the spine wall. The northern half contained a suite of two rooms for the laird one above the other and a kitchen with a huge fireplace, service stair to the cellars, and serving hatch to a western lobby, with a living room above it. There were also four rooms in the attic.

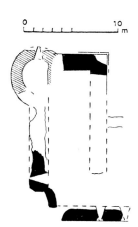

Plan of Couthally Castle

Outer Court at Craignethan

Sir James Hamilton was executed for treason in 1540 and after James V's death in 1542 Sir James' former ward the 2nd Earl of Arran, now Regent of Scotland for the infant Queen Mary, took possession of Craignethan. He was created Duke of Chatelherault in France in 1549 when Mary was betrothed to the Dauphin. When Mary took as her second husband Lord Darnley the Duke opposed the match. He fled to France and the Queen took over his castles of Craignethan and Cadzow. However he supported Mary's cause after her abdication in 1567 and helped in her escape2 from imprisonment at Loch Leven Castle. In 1568 Lord Claude Hamilton was defeated by Regent Moray at Langside and Cadzow and Craignethan had to be surrendered to the victor. Lord Claude recaptured both castles in 1568, and in 1570 the Hamiltons had Regent Moray shot in Edinburgh. Sporadic warfare between the Hamiltons and the Protestant party of the infant James VI continued until a treaty was signed in February 1573. Proclamations were issued against the Hamiltons in 1579 and levies were raised to captured Cadzow and Craignethan, although in the end they were surrendered without a fight, Lord John and Lord Claude going into exile. The castles were then made useless as fortresses. At Craignethan the great western screen wall was tumbled into the ditch in front burying the caponier which was only discovered again in 1962. The NE tower was also destroyed although the tower house appears to have remained habitable.

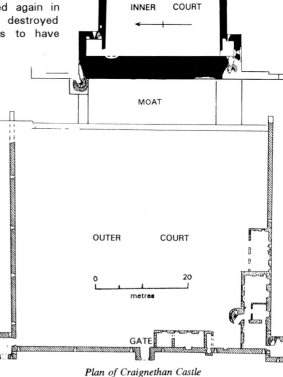

The caponier at Craignethan   *Plan of Craignethan Castle*

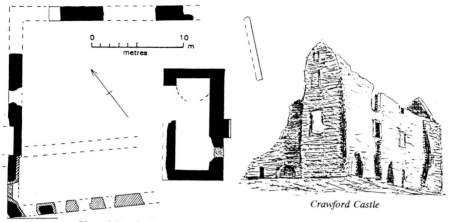

Crawford Castle

Plan of Crawford Castle

At some period between 1540 and 1579 a large outer court had been built to the west. It was not very defensible, being overlooked by a hillock immediately to the west, but gunports allowing a token show of strength are provided in the walls and in the central gateway and square corner towers of the west front. There are marks of intended ranges abutting again the inside of the walls. The castle custodian uses a two storey house in the SW corner built by the Covenanter Andrew Hay, who purchased Craignethan from the Duchess of Hamilton in 1659 and probably found the tower house by then uninhabitable. The date 1665 appears over the entrance in a round staircase turret. The SW tower was heightened and made part of this house. In 1730 Craignethan was purchased by the Duke of Douglas and it later passed to the Earls of Home who handed custody of it over to the State in 1949.

CRAWFORD   NS 954214

A castle here is recorded in 1175-8 although the motte and bailey earthworks may be a generation older than that. The castle controlled access from England and Dumfriesshire into the upper Clyde valley and has an alternative name of Tower Lindsay from the family of that name, created Earls of Crawford in the mid 15th century. They had held the barony from the 13th century but lost it in 1488 when James IV granted Crawford to Archibald, Earl of Angus. The Earl of Angus was forfeited in 1528 and the castle was used by James V as a hunting seat until his death in 1542, after which it was returned to the Earl. Crawford later went to the Hamilton Douglases, being sold to the Marquis of Douglas in c1600. For many years previous to that the Carmichaels of Meadowflat had been hereditary custodians. In the 18th century the lands were sold to Sir George Colebrooke.

The large low motte is covered with trees and has a surrounding ditch much silted up and slight remains of a quadrangular bailey platform 45m by 33m on the SW towards the river. A wall 1.6m thick of uncertain date and now very fragmentary surrounded a court 20m square on the motte. There seems to have once been a tower projecting on the NW side. A tower-like range 11.8m long and 6.6m wide of two storeys and an attic over a vaulted cellar was built against the SE side in the 16th century. A breast was provided to contain the fireplace of the hall, where the walling thins to just 1m. In the 17th century a SW range was provided with large windows in a new outer wall. Footings of the older wall then removed on that side can be seen.

CROOKSTON   A.M.*   NS 524624

Crookston is named after Robert de Croc who had an earth and timber castle here in the 12th century. The estate was purchased by Sir Alan Stewart in 1330 and was granted in 1361 to John Stewart of Darnley. His descendant built the mighty tower house within the older earthworks in the 1400s. The most famous of this branch of the Stewarts was Henry, Lord Darnley, who became the second husband of Mary, Queen of Scots and was murdered in 1567 when his house of Kirk O'Field near Edinburgh was blown up probably at the instigation of Patrick Hepburn, Earl of Bothwell. The castle later passed to the Maxwells of Pollock and is now in state care. The tower forms a landmark on a hill left as an open area beside White Cart water beside the Pollock housing estates. A ditch and outer bank with an entrance on the west surround a D-shaped platform sloping to the west and north and measuring 90m by 55m. There are traces of buildings in the SE corner not far from the tower.

The tower is 19m long by 12m wide and has side walls which at the level of the rib-vaulted basement are above a double chamfered plinth 3.2m thick on the south and 3.7m thick on the north. The latter wall contains the entrance which was closed by a portcullis and two sets of doors. From the passage rises a straight mural staircase rising over a square well chamber. The basement was lighted only by narrow loops in embrasures with steeply stepped cills. Leading off it are doorways into the lowest rooms of rectangular corner towers varying in size and shape. The NE tower is about 6m square and contains a vaulted prison entered only by a hatch in the floor of a guard room above which is reached by a narrow stair from the entrance passage. The west end of the building is very ruined and the two towers there have been destroyed, 19th century repairs having obscured even their joins with the main block. Doorways to them have been blocked up, the double doors to the NW tower suggesting that it contained in addition to a cellar a service stair connecting with the lobby in the hall NW corner to which the main stair led. This end of the hall would have been screened off with service rooms in the towers. The hall was a noble apartment 8.3m high to the crown of the now-destroyed pointed vault. At the east end is a fireplace in the end wall and a window in each sidewall. Seats high off the floor in the embrasures must have been reached by central steps now cut away. From the northern embrasure the portcullis was operated. In the SE corner is a staircase giving access to a private room in the tower beyond, to two upper rooms in each eastern tower, and to the lord's suite of living room and bedroom over the hall. Another stair at the west end would have served four more upper rooms in the towers at that end giving a total of at least nine private rooms in addition to the lord's suite. This is very ruined but has a fireplace and windows surviving at the east end. The top of the NE tower has been rebuilt, probably on the old lines, and now ends in corbel courses for a parapet with corner bartizans with machicolation slots on the outer sides.

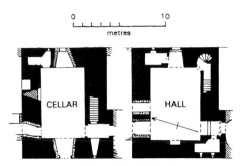

Plans of Dalzell Castle

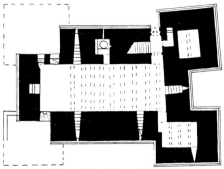

Plan of Crookston Castle

Dalzell Castle

Crookston Castle

CROSSBASKET NS 666559

The Lindsays of Mains Castle nearby to the west used this 16th century tower measuring 11.4m by 6.6m and set high above the wooded ravine of the Calder as a jointure house. Most of the windows of the three storeys have been enlarged and the quatrefoil and other shaped windows of the staircase are 19th century. Within the plain parapet on a single row of corbels is an attic with original small dormers.

DALZELL NS 756550

The barony of Dalzell was held by the family of that name from the 13th century until 1647. In the late 15th century they built a tower above the ravine of a tributary of the Clyde, which lies beyond the garden terraces to the south. The tower measures 11.7m by 9.7m and is 14.3m high from the ground above the ravine to the top of a parapet with roundels on a chequer arrangement of corbels. The south wall contains a straight stair from an entrance at the thickened west end of that side and then a spiral stair rises in the SE corner to end in a round caphouse. This lower entrance and another at hall level on the north side may have been later insertions as there is another doorway with a portcullis groove at hall level in the thickened section of the south wall. The lord's hall above is vaulted, and above is the lord's private room with several mural chambers. Beside the tower is a rectangular court with a round tower at the Sw corner and a dry moat crossed by modern bridges on the west. Buildings of the 1850s lie where there was probably another arm of the moat on the north side. The range on the south side connecting the corner tower with the keep is dated 1649 with the arms and initials of James Hamilton of Boggs who inherited the castle from the last Dalzell two years earlier and whose descendants used the castle until the 20th century. Parts of the range may be older as there seems to have been more than one kitchen, and it has a central bay of the 1850s facing south, opposite a corbelled out north staircase.

Dargarvel Castle

DARGARVEL   NS 433693

This building now lying within an army camp stands on flat ground by a burn 2km south of Bishopton. It consists of a 19th century mansion added to one corner of a Z-plan castle bearing on the east gable the Maxwell arms and the date 1584 (the 4 is the wrong way round). The main block is of three storeys with an attic in the roof and measures 13.7m by 7.2m. The staircase turret 4.3m in diameter at the SW corner is balanced by a second turret on the NE corner, both having conical roofs. An entrance on the south side leads into a passage connecting the stair with a kitchen and two cellars. Above are a hall and private room end to end and there are two bedrooms on the third storey. Access to the attics and to a top room over the main stair is by a stair in a turret carried on a chequer arrangement of corbels.

DOUGLAS   NS 842318

The castle here mentioned in 1288 may have been either or stone or wood. It was captured by Edward I but retaken by the Scots, being the scene of various bold adventures by Robert Bruce's friend Sir James Douglas. James II destroyed the castle after his defeat of the Black Douglases in 1455 but it was probably rebuilt not long afterwards. The single round ruined corner tower now standing on a site that would have accommodated a court about 40m square with a ditch on the two naturally weakest sides dates from about the time of the Dukedom of Douglas created in 1707 when the castle was declared to be its principal messuage. The building was destroyed by fire in 1755 and the tower left as a garden ornament for a new house now gone.

DUCHAL   NS 334685

Duchal belonged to the Lyles probably from the 13th century. Sir Robert Lyle was created a lord in the 1440s. He died c1470 and his heiress Margaret married Alexander Lyle of Craigbate. When their great-grandson John, 4th Lord Lyle died in 1544 his title passed to the descendants of his daughter Jean and her husband Sir Neil Montgomerie of Lainshaw although Duchal is said to have gone to the Porterfield family. There does not appear to be any evidence of the castle being occupied in the 16th and 17th centuries and it may have been a ruin since 1489 when James IV captured the castles of Crookston and Duchal with the aid of the celebrated cannon Mons Meg now on display in the vaults of Edinburgh Castle. The castle site is overlooked by higher ground but was difficult of access except on the west where there is now a lane for it is a promontory almost surrounded by the ravines of the Green Water and Blackett Water 2.5km SE of the former Kilmacolm station. Partly hidden among trees and undergrowth are fragments 4 to 5m high of a curtain wall enclosing an irregularly shaped area 55m long by 22m wide. The opening near the NW corner seems to have been a window serving a lean-to building. The gateway must have been on the west and there was a north postern reached by steps from inside and an east postern giving onto the point of the promontory. There are no remains of the curtain on the south side but there is here a knob of natural rock 4m high bearing the base of a tower about 12m by 10m over walling 2.5m thick. The tower and curtain could be of any date from the late 13th century to the mid 15th century.

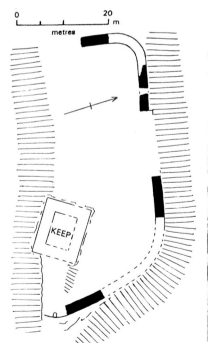

Plan of Duchall Castle

Later Tower on site of Douglas Castle

EASTEND NS 948375

This is a much altered and extended 16th or 17th century building on a flat site.

EASTSHIELD NS 960500

Only the end wall and a staircase turret 3m in diameter remain of the three storey tower of c1600 6m wide.

EDMONSTON NT 070422

The Douglases held Edmonston from 1322 until the then Earl of Douglas sold the estate c1650 to Baillie of Walston. In the early 18th century it was acquired by Laurence Brown and in 1867 it was sold to the Woodrops of Ellrickle and Dalmarnock. The three storey tower of c1600 measures 6.2m by 7.7m. The entrance lies beside a staircase turret 3m in diameter on the north corner. The cellar has a gunloop in the opposite wall. The tower stood roofless but intact until 1872 when it was blown up by a tenant who was afraid of it falling and the upper south corner is now missing. The last remnant of the hall fireplace fell c1890. A court adjoined to the north with an entrance facing east beside the tower. A house later built in the court was demolished in 1815 and a new house built lower down the slope.

ELLISTON NS 392598

Within the garden of a house on a shelf above the Black Cart Water 0.5km SW of Howood is an early 16th century tower measuring about 11.5m by 9.6m. There is now no access into the vaulted basement which is now filled up with rubble, and only one wall remains of the hall above. The SE end wall seems to have been thickened to contain mural chambers and probably also the entrance and staircase. On this side between the tower and house are foundations of the NE and SE walls of a small court.

Plan of Elliston Castle

Edmonston Castle

Elliston Castle

FARME   NS 620627

The Stewarts or the Crawfurds built the three storey 16th century tower which stood at a corner of a later mansion above the Clyde near Rutherglen. The attic lay within a parapet on a single row of corbels and there were large later inserted windows.

FATLIPS   NS 968341

On a slight shelf 370m up on the south side of Scaut Hill west of Symington are remains of the basement of a 16th century tower 11.5m long by 8.5m wide over walling 2m thick. This storey was divided into two, one section being presumably a kitchen as it has a fireplace. No entrance or stair survive, and it is likely that there was a doorway at hall level on the south side where the ground level was highest.

GARRION   NS 797512

The four storey L-plan tower by the junction of the Garrion Burn and the Clyde dates from about the time of a charter of 1605 confirming James Hamilton and Elizabeth Hay in possession of Garrion, which the Hamiltons had formerly held from the archbishops of Glasgow. The tower measures only 7.5m by 5.8m but despite this the third storey seems to have always been divided into two bedrooms with fireplaces in the end walls. They now open off an extension rather than directly from the staircase in the wing, the well of which is square at the bottom. There are shot-holes below the window sills. The tower was restored from ruin and extended in the 19th century.

GILBERTFIELD   NS 653588

This L-plan ruin above the Clyde Valley near Cambuslang is dated 1607. It has a wing big enough to contain a tier of rooms in addition to a wide staircase in a square well. The main block measures 11.5m by 6.7m and contains a kitchen and wine cellar with a service stair to the hall above. Above are two storeys of bedrooms, the uppermost having closets in bartizans on the NW and SE corners of the wing and main block. Much of the east gable containing the kitchen fireplace flue fell c1950.

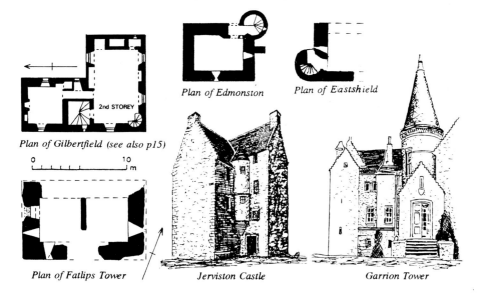

Plan of Gilbertfield (see also p15)

Plan of Edmonston

Plan of Eastshield

Plan of Fatlips Tower

Jerviston Castle

Garrion Tower

GREENOCK

Part of the building overlooking the Clyde, which was entirely destroyed in 1886 for building the Caledonian Railway, was presumably the "auld castellsteid, castell, tour, fortalice, and manor place new buildit" mentioned in a charter of 1540. This document transferred the estate from the recently forfeited and executed Sir James Hamilton to Sir Alexander Shaw of Sauchie. Sir Alexander then transferred Greenock to his eldest son John in 1542. A well was dated 1629 with the initials of John Shaw, laird from 1620 to 1679, and his wife Helen Houston. The back entrance was dated 1637, the staircase doorway bore the year 1674, and the garden entrance was dated 1635. The house began to decay in the time of Sir John Shaw, who died in 1699. In the 1730s Lady Cathcart had a fine new house built on the western part of the site but in 1745 the family moved to Ardgowan after which the house at Greenock was sub-let to tenants and the cellars were at one time used as a prison.

The architectural history of the house was complex and is difficult to unravel from the plans and drawing which have survived. The eastern part may have incorporated part of a 15th century tower. At the time of demolition the house was a gabled structure with a wing projecting west from the SW corner and a stair turret in the re-entrant angle. Another wing projected both east and south from the SE corner. Only a tiny court divided the house from the later mansion. This had a symmetrical west facade grafted onto the remains of the original 1.6m thick courtyard wall.

HAGGS   A.M.*   NS 560626

A cable moulding surrounds the doorway and a pair of blank panels above. The inscription between these panels and the doorway tells us the house was built in 1585 by Sir John Maxwell of Pollock and his wife Dame Margaret Conyngham. It was restored from ruin in the 19th century after use as a smithy, the north wall having been breached to give better access to the basement containing the usual two cellars with a passage running past them to a kitchen at the far end from the main stair in the wing. The main block is 7.2m wide and 17m long, enough to contain a private room beyond the hall. At that level ends the main stair in the wing, which was originally round fronted. Two other stairs are then corbelled out over the re-entrant angle and in the middle of the adjacent south front. The latter is set upon ornate corbelling and interrupts a horizontal cable moulding round the main block. Another moulding runs round at eaves level. The building now contains a museum of childhood.

HALLBAR   NS 836470

An act of Parliament of 1581 ratifying a grant of lands here to Harie Stewart, brother-in-law of the Earl of Arran, describes this little tower as the fortalice of the barony of Braidwood. The tower was probably built about a generation earlier and occupies half the neck of a promontory beside the Tiddler Burn above its confluence with the Auchenglen Burn and then the Clyde. There are the barest traces of a former court 30m by 13m with a wall 1.3m thick. The tower measures 7.5m over walls 1.6m thick. It contains a vaulted cellar, a hall over, a private room for the laird, and two upper storeys. The three lower levels are connected by straight lengths of stair. Another stair then leads up to one of two lengths of wall-walk flanking and giving access to the topmost room. This room has an oriel window on three corbels towards the court. It has a machicolation defending the doorway. On the other side is a doorway which led to a timber brattice giving access to a dovecot consisting of nesting boxes set into the outer wall-face. There are doorways into the cellar and into the hall from the former barmkin wall-walk. Hallbar was acquired by Sir George Lockhart of Lee c1662 and the tower was kept in repair by his descendants, being reroofed in the late 19th century.

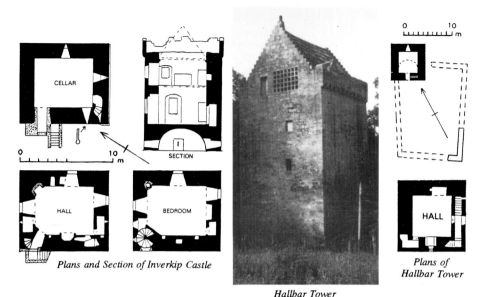

Plans and Section of Inverkip Castle

Plans of
Hallbar Tower

Hallbar Tower

HOUSTON   NS 412672

The 16th century mansion of the Stewart Earls of Lennox on a rise east of the church had four ranges around a court with a high tower at the Nw corner and two turrets on the south side where the entrance probably lay. The estate was later purchased by a Captain Macrae who in 1780 pulled down the north, west, and south ranges offering the materials to the villagers on condition that they transferred their houses to a discreet distance to the west. In 1782 The Spiers of Elderslie acquired Houston and modernised the remaining range for use as a shooting lodge. In the 1870s they made considerable additions to the south and east. The surviving ancient range is 24m long by 7m wide and has an east wall 1.8m thick surmounted by continuous corbelled courses for a former parapet but now supporting the eaves of the roof. The internal subdivisions of the range are much altered, only one thick crosswall being original. The entrance doorway on the west side giving onto a scale-and-platt staircase has pilasters with the date 1625 and the prayer: The.Blessings.Of.God.Rest.Vpon.This.Hovse. And.Familie.Macking.Us.To.Dae.Thy.Will.O.Lord.For.The.Just.Lives.By.Faith.

INVERKIP   NS 205728

This Stewart tower of c1500 stands on a cliff within the estate of a modern mansion to the NE. The vaulted basement has loops with a bottom roundel and was originally reached only by a service stair in the SW corner. A 17th century wing added in front of the original entrance at the foot of the main staircase at hall level has been destroyed. A modern stair now leads to this upper entrance, although at the same time a doorway, now blocked, was forced through underneath it into the cellar. The hall has three wide windows and two small closets in the walls. The inserted corner fireplace supplementing the one in the west wall suggests the room was later divided. Above is a private room with a fireplace and latrine in the south wall and three large windows, and there was an attic within the wall-walk. The parapet is supported on a chequer arrangement of corbels and has roundels or bartizans at three of the corners.

JERVISTON   NS 760581

Jerviston was a Baillie seat and lies above the Clyde south of Motherwell. It is an L-plan tower of c1600 measuring 9.5m by 6.6m with the wing containing a wide spiral stair from the entrance to the hall, and then a smaller stair is corbelled out in the re-entrant angle. This stair has lost its original conical roof and a bartizan on the adjacent corner of the main block has also been removed except for the bottom course of corbelling. The entrance has a large moulding and an inscription now nearly obliterated plus initials of Robert Baillie and Elizabeth Hamilton.

JERVISWOOD   NS 884455

This castle lies on a high promontory above the south side of the River Mouse near Lanark. Beside the last remnants of a 15th century tower of the Livingstones is a three storey L-plan house erected by the Edinburgh merchant George Baillie after he acquired the estate in 1636. The wing overlaps two sides of the main block and there are gables in the middles of the long sides as well as at the ends, but there are no turrets.

JOHNSTONE   NS 425623

Originally called Easter Cochrane after the original owners, this L-plan 15th century tower was renamed, extended, and gothicised after being purchased by the Hunters of Johnstone in 1733. By 1830 it formed just part of a large mansion but the rest was all removed c1950, the tower being left to serve as a local authority store.

LAMINGTON   NS 980320

Marion Bradfute, heiress of the 13th century owner of Lamington was taken off to Lanark by Hazelrig, Edward I's governor of the town and castle there. She became the wife of William Wallace and was killed by the English after helping her husband to escape from pursuit, and being avenged by a massacre of the English garrison at Lanark. Supposedly descended from her were the Baillies of Lamington, later lords Lamington. Parts of the south and west walls of their 15th century tower 11.7m long by 9.6m wide lie on a small wooded hillock near the flat near bank of the Clyde. The

destroyed walls contained the entrance and staircase and the only surviving features are a western basement loop, a blocked south window at hall level, and a fragment of the SE corner bartizan reset far below its original position as the wall now stands only 7m high. A fragment of the NW bartizan which was still in situ on the building a century ago now lies in an adjacent field.

Jerviswood Castle

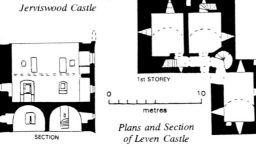

1st STOREY

0   10
metres

SECTION

*Plans and Section
of Leven Castle*

HALL

2nd STOREY

STAIR

KITCHEN

FIREPLACE

Leven Castle

Mains Castle

LANARK NS 878434

The name Castle Bank must refer to the vanished castle which may have been of wood and does not seem to have been rebuilt after destruction by the Bruces.

LEVEN NS 216764

This castle by a stream behind a hotel above the Clyde estuary was restored in the 1980s. It was built by the Mortons c1500, passed to the Sempills in 1547, and later went to the Shaw Stewarts. It is composed of two rectangular blocks measuring 10.6m by 7.9m and 8m by 6.3m which only touch each other at one corner which contains the main staircase. The wing contains a kitchen with a wide fireplace over a cellar with a bedroom on top and is thought to be a slightly later addition, although the parapets with chequered corbelling and roundels of both parts seem to be one work. The main block has two cellars each with a service stair to the hall, and a pair of bedrooms on top, and both parts have extra attic rooms in the roofs. From the head of the wine cellar service stair rises a secondary spiral stair serving the bedroom at the west end. Before restoration the entrance was half buried with earth and debris and parts of the kitchen wing east wall had gone.

MAINS NS 627560

The Lindsays of Dunrod acquired Kilbride in 1382 and lived in great state at Mains until they sold it in the late 17th century. The roof of the early 16th century tower was removed in 1723 and the later ranges accompanying it were allowed to decay. According to old descriptions there was a surrounding deep ditch crossed by a drawbridge on the east to a gate with the royal arms above it. Traces of an older castle to the north were visible in the 19th century. The tower was then re-roofed and it is still habitable, a new parapet having now been built on the original corbelling 12.5m above ground. The tower measures 11.2m by 8m and has a basement and sleeping loft below a vault, a hall above, and two rooms on the fourth storey. The west wall contains the staircase and mural chambers including a prison reached by a hatch from the room at loft level. This wall is not thicker than the others and does not contain the entrance, which is round the corner in the south wall. There is a slab roof over the stairhead contained in a caphouse or turret. The hall and bedrooms have latrines in the north wall and retain their original narrow windows. See plan p144.

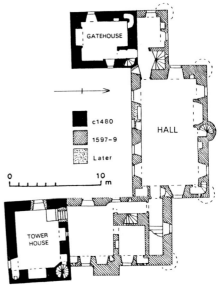

Mearns Castle

Plan of Newark Castle

MEARNS   NS 553553

On a rock above the town of Newton Mearns is a tower house built by Herbert, Lord Maxwell under the terms of a licence granted in 1449 by James II. In the mid 17th century Robert Maxwell, Earl of Nithsdale sold it to his kinsman George Maxwell of Nether Pollock, but soon afterwards it passed to the Shaw Stewarts. It was a ruin by the 19th century but has been restored to contain rooms serving a round church built next to it on the edge of the crag in 1971, the building being connected by narrow corridors at the level of the vaulted cellar and the very lofty vaulted hall above. The bedroom storey on top is now covered by a flat modern roof. Only the triple stepped corbels remain of a machicolated parapet. The cellar has two loops, a straight service stair to the hall, and a 17th century doorway to the outside. The round arched original entrance above at hall level is now partly blocked. It has a drawbar slot and is flanked by a mural room and the main stair, onto which the service stair leads. The hall has the usual fireplace at the far end with a window with seats nearby in each sidewall. A window high up over the entrance is thought to have served as a musicians' gallery reached from the staircase.

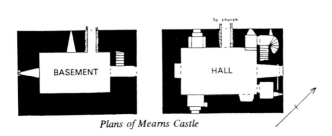

Plans of Mearns Castle

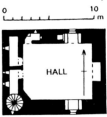

Plan of Mains Castle

MONKLAND   NS 730633

This house lies in the Calder Valley near Airdrie. It consists of a main block 19m long which has three storeys and an attic at the east end but is a storey higher at the west end. It is set against a bank so that the entrance on the north side is at second storey level. It leads into a staircase turret in a re-entrant angle between the main block and a square wing on the NW corner which contains the kitchen in its lowest level. On the southern corners are round turrets. Evidence of the late date of this building is the lack of a large hall, the main block having instead a central lobby with a dining room and drawing room of equal size on either side. A modern porch now covers the entrance and most of the windows have been enlarged in the 18th and 19th centuries.

NEWARK   A.M.*   NS 331745

Newark Castle lies hidden among the factories and docklands of Port Glasgow. The original "new wark" erected by George Maxwell soon after being given the barony of Finlaystone by his father John Maxwell of Calderwood in 1478 is a four storey tower house 8.7m by 6.9m. By 1495, when James IV paid a visit on his way to the Western Isles, a rectangular court had been added to the west with a three storey gatehouse tower at the far end. Except for a round flanking turret forming a dovecot facing the river the courtyard walls have long gone but the two towers survive now joined together by a mansion with a symmetrical front to the river. This building bears the dates 1597 and 1599 and the initials of its builder Patrick Maxwell. He was involved in the murder of his neighbours Patrick Maxwell of Stanely and the Montgomerie Earl of Eglinton in 1584 and 1596 respectively during a series of feuds which also involved the Crichtons, the Montgomeries of Skelmorie, and the Maxwells of Calderwood. In his old age he maltreated his wife Margaret Crawfurd who had borne him 16 children. He became a J.P. in 1623, as did his son in 1636, and in 1662 the then laird was the judge at witchcraft trials at Greenock and Inverkip. In 1668 George Maxwell, a noted merchant trader, sold land in the barony to the burgesses of Glasgow for the construction of the port facilities which became known as Port Glasgow. In the late 19th century the building was decayed and only inhabited by several poor families. It has been restored by the Scottish Office and a custodian now lives in the east wing.

Monkland Castle

Newark Castle

Patrick Maxwell's mansion has a block 14.2m long by 8m wide with at each end of the south wide a wing connecting respectively with the tower house and the gatehouse. The entrance is commanded by a few shotholes and has above it the inscription "The Blessingis Of God Be Herin". The entrance leads into a small lobby in the east wing from which a scale-and-platt stair leads up to the hall, while passages lead off to a kitchen, food store and wine cellar under the hall, a bakehouse in the east wing, and to the cellar in the base of the tower house, plus two other small stores tucked away in corners. The hall has a noble fireplace similar to that at Spedlin's Tower in Dumfriesshire. There are service stairs down to the kitchen and wine cellar. Other chambers at this level are a living room and a small room in the east wing, the original main living room or hall of the tower house, and a living room over the gateway with a service area next to it in the NW corner. Access to the third storey is by a wide stair in the east wing and by a turret set in the middle of the north front. Timber walls divided the main space into four bedrooms, and there was a fifth bedroom in the gatehouse, plus two rooms in the east wing and two more, one above the other, in the old tower. The tower house has its own staircase connecting all its rooms and has windows with pedimented heads inserted in its west wall to match those of the mansion. The gateway passage has a south loop with a bottom roundel which formerly flanked the courtyard wall and has a guard room on the north side.

OLD BISHOPTON   NS 422717

In the late 17th century John Brisbane disposed of the estate long held by his family to John Walkinshaw. It was later sold to Hugh Dunlop and then passed by marriage to Lord Sempill from whom it was acquired by Sir James Maxwell of Pollock. The existing house is a plain L-planned 17th century building now much altered and extended. The wing containing the rusticated doorway and a scale-and-platt stair serving all three storeys is 6.6m wide and projects 3.7m from a block 13m long by 7.4m wide. Two of the cellars have vaults and original narrow loops.

PATRICKHOLM   NS 756500

The ruined house and outbuildings above a bend of the Avon opposite Larkhall are mostly 19th century but incorporate a 17th century cellar vaulted with long thin stones. It has doorways to the east and west and altered windows to north and south.

POLLOCK   NS 522570

On the end of a rocky ridge west of Newton Mearns with extensive views to the east, west, and north is a mansion which once had on the pediments of dormer windows the dates 1686 and 1687 with the initials of Sir Robert Pollock and his wives Annabella Maxwell and Annabella Stewart, while the courtyard gateway to the west was dated 1694. The SW wing incorporates the north and west walls of a tower house 9m square built c1500. These walls contain a straight stair to the second storey and then a spiral stair leading up in the corner. The house was gutted by fire in 1882 but was restored in the 1890s for Mrs Fergusson Pollok under the direction of the architect Charles Johnston. This was a pollock seat as early as the 12th century.

POLNOON   NS 586513

On the end of a ridge above the Dunwan Burn 1.3km SE of Eaglesham crossroads is a low tree-clad motte. Massive tumbled fragments of an early tower house upon it may represent the castle built here in 1388 by Sir John Montgomerie. Polnoon was one of the residences of Hew Montgomerie, 3rd Earl of Eglinton mentioned in his contract of 1568 with the Glasgow "glassin wricht" (glazier) George Elphinstone.

PROVAN   NS 668663

Since 1935 the Scottish National Trust has administered the 16th century house and court of the Baillies who obtained the lands from the Archbishop of Glasgow. The house has a kitchen and two cellars connected only by a hatch to a hall and private room above, being reached by an outside stair. There are servants' rooms in the roof and there is a round tower in the NE corner. Steps lead up to a lookout place with shot-holes over the courtyard gateway. On the wall are the date 1677 and initials of Sir Patrick Hamilton, whose predecessor Sir Robert married a Baillie heiress.

RANFORLIE   NS 384652

John Knox, the celebrated mid 16th century Protestant preacher and thorn in the side of Queen Mary, is the best known member of the family who held Ranforlie from at least the 15th century until 1665 when the barony was alienated to William Cochrane, 1st Earl of Dundonald. It later passed to the Aikenheads. On an eminence by a stream above Bridge of Weir and with a golf course on the level ground to the east are the lower two storeys of a tower measuring 7.8m by 6.7m probably of the early 16th century. There are two superimposed entrances in the south end of the 1.4m thick NE wall. A spiral stair led up from the higher level in the east corner. The NW wall is missing. Among bushes and trees to the south are fragments of a small court with a range of three cellars on the SE side above which was probably a hall. There are footings of other rooms to the east of the tower.

RENFREW   NS 507682

On Castle Hill between the town and the Clyde are slight traces of earthworks of a castle built by Walter Fitz-Alan who was granted the estate by David I and confirmed in it by Malcolm IV in 1157. There is nothing to suggest that the Stewarts, descendants of Fitz-Alan, rebuilt the castle in stone although Robert III made the town a royal burgh in 1396 and in 1494 created his eldest son James Baron Renfrew, a title still borne by the present Prince of Wales.

SHIELDHILL   NT 006405

This much altered building on the north side of Biggar Common is now a hotel.

Old Bishopton

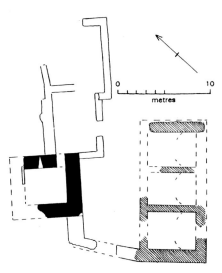

Plan of Ranforlie Castle

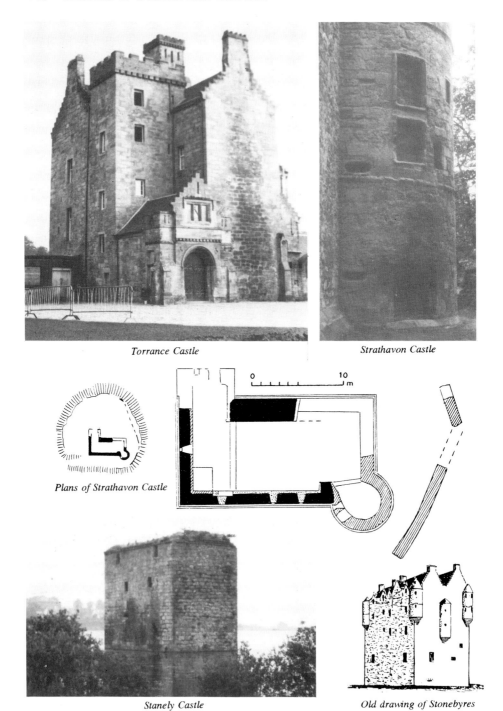

Torrance Castle

Strathavon Castle

Plans of Strathavon Castle

Stanely Castle

Old drawing of Stonebyres

SNAR   NS 863201

By a bend of the Snar Water at Snar Farm 4km SW of Crawfordjohn are slight remains of a room about 3m square with walling 1m thick which was an adjunct to a rectangular building which was perhaps an outbuilding of a 16th century tower.

STANELY   NS 464616

The barony of Stanely belonged to the Danzielstones in the 14th century but passed by marriage to the Maxwells of Calderwood, and then to the Maxwells of Newark who built the present tower c1500. It has been standing in a reservoir since 1837. The estate, now mostly built over, was sold to Dame Jean Hamilton, Lady Ross of Hawkhead in 1629 and was later held by the Earl of Glasgow who married her daughter. The castle has main block 14m long by 7.2m wide with a basement currently under water and three upper storeys connected by a staircase in a wing 6m square. Only the continuous corbelled courses survive of the former parapets.

STONEBYRES   NS 853440

The castle of the Veres, lairds of Stonebyres from the 15th century until c1850 was encased in a mansion soon after it changed hands. It consisted of a 15th century tower 10m by 8.7m over walls up to 2.7m thick which was in the 16th century incorporated into a block 20.7m long with a gunport in the furthest of several new cellars. A stair in one corner of the new part connected the hall 9.6m long with that cellar, and then a stair in a turret projected from the end wall led up to the third storey room at that end, the other bedrooms being served by the original stair of the old tower. At the corners were round bartizans with closets serving both the third and fourth storeys. The double gabled roof had side gables and many dormer windows.

STRATHAVON   NS 701447

Strathavon or Avondale Castle was built by Andrew Stewart, an illegitimate grandson of the second Duke of Albany, who obtained the barony in 1457 and was recognised as Lord Avondale. It is strongly sided on a natural mound with steep falls on three sides to the Powmillan Burn. Only fragments remain of the surrounding barmkin. The main block north wall still stands complete although except for the outer openings of three basement loops all the features have been obscured by unsightly modern concrete patching, and there is a high and thick fragment of the south wall. A splayed plinth continues all round so it appears the building was always as big as its present size of 21.2m by 11.2m. Probably the second storey contained a hall and private room end to end, a "palace" rather than a tower house arrangement. The square stair wing now reduced to footings may be original but the round tower at the diagonally opposite corner is 16th century. It has gunports and blank panels above an entrance which is impossibly low to be in its original state. It cannot have had a higher head, yet it does not appear to have had a lower threshold as a plinth continues below.

THE PEEL   NS 362587

In a very inaccessible position on a thickly overgrown peninsular in Castle Semple Loch 1km east of Lochwinoch is the lower part of an ashlar faced tower of c1480-1530.

TORRANCE   NS 825484

A crenellated staircase turret one storey high has been added within the re-entrant angle of the plain L-plan tower built by the Hamiltons c1605. It passed in the mid 18th century to the Stewarts of Castlemilk. Among further alterations is the addition of a gabled one storey porch in front of the entrance doorway in the staircase turret.

WANDEL   NS 952288

The Tower or Bower of Wandel now comprises the very ruined and defaced basement of a 15th century tower on a mound in a good defensive position above a bend of the upper section of the Clyde. The tower measured 8.5m by 5.6m and had a vaulted cellar with north, west and south loops in walls up to 2.5m thick. The entrance and stair were in the destroyed SE corner.

WAYGATESHAW   NS 825484

It was probably Alexander Lockhart who married a Murray heiress in 1539 who built a tower on the north side of the Clyde near Carluke. The tower contains a vaulted hall over a pair of vaulted cellars with gunports and now has just one storey above, but was originally higher. The stair wing is a 17th century addition. The tower lies in the NW corner of a court entered through a segmental arched and roll moulded gateway flanked by gunports and surmounted by a carved lion and two dogs. There are ranges of various later periods within the court. The building was restored in the 1980s.

WESTHALL   NT 048473

By the roadside in front of the farm are remains of a small L-planned tower of c1600 with a main block 9.2m long by 5.8m wide over walls 1.1m thick. The wing presumably contained the entrance and staircase. The only features are traces of the cellar vault and of a fireplace or window in the living room west wall.

WEST SHIELD   NS 946494

In the 17th century the Lockharts of Lee lengthened a house with three vaulted cellars built by the Denholms in the late 16th century. they also added a wing and a stair turret in the re-entrant angle thus created. The house now lies roofed but derelict.

LIST OF EARTHWORKS

ABINGTON NS 933250 Ditch 2m deep divides pear shaped mound summit 22m by 11m above the Clyde from a D-shaped bailey 75m by 55m with a rampart 1m high. CARNWATH NS 974467 Fine tree-clad motte of classic inverted pudding bowl shape 9m high to summit 15m across on the golf course west of the village.

CASTLEHEAD NS 475632 Late medieval pottery was found in the excavation of this probable ringwork near Paisley.

COULTER A.M. NT 019364 Mound above wide bend of Clyde rising 4m above lane to summit 12m across. It is less high on the other sides.

ELVANFOOT NS 951186 Mound and bailey on north side of Collins Burn 1km north of the village. The site commands a bend of the upper Clyde Valley.

HAMILTON NS 716566 A mound lies NE of the town, by the M74, south of Clyde.

KILMACOLM NS 358683 Mound 2m high on east, 4m high to NW, with summit 14m across above the River Gryfe 1.5km south of the village.

MAINS NS 628561 Motte immediately NE of tower may be castle mentioned in 1190.

NEILSTON Documents of the 1180s refer to a castle here.

ROBERTON NS 940271 Mound 2.5m high to summit 12 across by bend of Clyde. Damaged in the 1960s when cut away to make a silage pit for Moat Farm. The name refers to Robert the Fleming, an early 12th century tenant here. A possible alternative site for his seat is the earthwork on the hillside north of the village.

WESTON NS 826294 The north half of a mound 3m high and 15m across on top has been eroded away by the Douglas Water. Predecessor of nearby Douglas Castle.

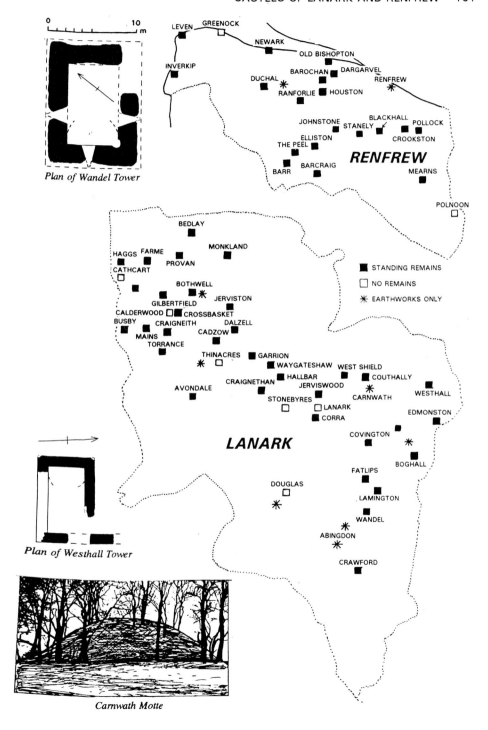

Plan of Wandel Tower

0   10 m

LEVEN GREENOCK
INVERKIP
NEWARK
OLD BISHOPTON
BAROCHAN   DARGARVEL
DUCHAL
RANFORLIE   HOUSTON   RENFREW
JOHNSTONE   STANELY   BLACKHALL   POLLOCK
ELLISTON   CROOKSTON
THE PEEL
BARR   BARCRAIG   MEARNS

RENFREW

POLNOON

BEDLAY
HAGGS FARME   MONKLAND
CATHCART   PROVAN
BOTHWELL
GILBERTFIELD   JERVISTON
CALDERWOOD   CROSSBASKET
BUSBY   CRAIGNEITH   DALZELL
MAINS   CADZOW
TORRANCE
THINACRES   GARRION
WAYGATESHAW   WEST SHIELD
CRAIGNETHAN   HALLBAR   COUTHALLY
JERVISWOOD
AVONDALE   CARNWATH   WESTHALL
STONEBYRES
LANARK   EDMONSTON
CORRA
COVINGTON
FATLIPS   BOGHALL
DOUGLAS
LAMINGTON
WANDEL
ABINGDON
CRAWFORD

LANARK

■ STANDING REMAINS
□ NO REMAINS
✳ EARTHWORKS ONLY

Plan of Westhall Tower

Carnwath Motte

FURTHER READING

A History of Scotland, Rosalind Mitchison, London, 1970
Ayrshire: Its History and Historic Families, Vol 1, Robertson, Kilmarnock, 1908.
Castles, Plantagenet Somerset Fry, David & Charles, 1980.
Castles and Mansions of Ayrshire, A.H. Millar, Edinburgh, 1885.
Discovering Scottish Castles, Mike Salter, Shire, 1985.
Homelands of the Clans, Gerald Warner, Collins 1980.
Medieval Archeology (published annually).
Norman Castles in Britain, Derek Renn, Baker, 1974
Portrait of the Burns Country, Hugh Douglas, London 1968
Proceedings of The Society of Antiquaries of Scotland.
Royal Commission on Ancient and Historical Monuments inventories for Wigtownshire
    (1912), The Stewartry of Kirkcudbright (1914), and Dumfries-shire (1920).
Scotland from the Earliest Times, W. Croft Dickinson, Oxford, 1961.
The Castellated and Domestic Architecture of Scotland 5 vols, David McGibbon and
    Thomas Ross, David Douglas 1883-92. Facsimile reprint James Thin 1977.
The Castles of Scotland, Maurice Lindsay, Constable, 1986.
The Fortified House in Scotland Vol 4, Nigel Tranter, Oliver & Boyd, 1966.
The Scottish Castle, Stewart Cruden, Nelson, 1960.
Transactions of the Dumfries and Galloway Natural History and Archeological Society.
Transactions of the Glasgow Archeological Society.
The Scottish Office (now Historic Scotland) has produced individual guides to
    Crossraguel Abbey, Lincluden College, and the castles of Bothwell, Cardoness,
    Craignethan, Maclellan's and Threave.
The National Trust has produced a guide for Culzean Castle.

OTHER CASTLES WHICH EXISTED IN SW SCOTLAND

These have all been destroyed or rebuilt almost out of existance.

Ayrshire - Auchendrane, Barbieston, Blackcraig, Bradan, Brockloch, Gilmour,
    Kirkmichael, Knockdon, Ladyland, Lochrig, Montgreenan, Newton, Robert, Ryehill,
    Sauchrie, Skeldon, Tarbet, Trochrague.

Dumfries - Arkland, Auchengassel, Brydekirk, Calfield, Cockpool, Craigs, Dalveen,
    Durrisdeer, Gilmour, Hallguards, Harelaw, Kirkpatrick, Kirton, Newbie, Raffles,
    Redhall, Runstonfoote, Sark, Snade, Stonehouse, Wauchope, Westhills.

Galloway - Appleby, Auchlane, Auchenfranco, Balcary, Barmeal, Craigcoch, Cutreoch,
    Garthland, Greenlaw, Larg, Manor, Machermore, Mindork, Muirfad.

Lanark & Renfrew - Allarton, Auchenbathie, Auchenames, Auldhouse, Belstane,
    Beltrees, Carnbroe, Cleghorn, Cloak, Cot, Crawfordjohn, Drumry, Dunrod, Dunsyre,
    Duntervy, Gilkerscleugh, Gourock, Gryffe, Hallcraig, Hawkhead, Inchnock, Kirton of
    Carluke, Lickprivick, Ogs, Parkhall, Plotcock, Ringsdale, Rutherglen, Valance.

The outer court at Cadzow